WITHDRAWN

Heavenly
Miracles

Other books by
Jamie C. Miller, Laura Lewis, and Jennifer Basye Sander

Christmas Miracles

The Magic of Christmas Miracles

Mothers' Miracles

A Gift of Miracles

Heavenly Miracles

MAGICAL TRUE STORIES OF GUARDIAN ANGELS AND ANSWERED PRAYERS

Jamie C. Miller, Laura Lewis, and
Jennifer Basye Sander

WILLIAM MORROW
An Imprint of HarperCollins*Publishers*

A Big City Books Idea

HEAVENLY MIRACLES. Copyright © 2000 by Jamie C. Miller, Laura Lewis, and Jennifer Basye Sander.

For information address HarperCollins Publishers Inc.,
10 East 53rd Street, New York, NY 10022.

HarperCollins books may be purchased for educational, business, or sales promotional use. For information please write: Special Markets Department, HarperCollins Publishers Inc., 10 East 53rd Street, New York, NY 10022.

FIRST EDITION

Designed by JoAnne Metsch

Printed on acid-free paper

Library of Congress Cataloging-in-Publication Data
Heavenly miracles : magical true stories of guardian angels and answered prayers / [edited by] Jamie C. Miller, Laura Lewis, and Jennifer Basye Sander.— 1st. ed.
    p.   cm.
ISBN 0-688-17370-5
1. Miracles.   2. Guardian angels.   3. Prayer.   I. Miller, Jamie C.
II. Lewis, Laura, 1963–   III. Sander, Jennifer Basye, 1958– .

BL487 .H43   2000
291.2'117—dc21   00-038926

00   01   02   03   04   QW   10   9   8   7   6   5   4   3   2   1

To Pete, Olivia, and Evan
with love

To Laura,
for giving us a piece of heaven on earth

There is no winter harsh enough
to withhold the promise of spring.

—KAREN KAISER CLARKE

Contents

Contents

Heavenly
Miracles

INTRODUCTION

miracle n. 1. An event that seems impossible to explain by natural laws and so is regarded as supernatural in origin or as an act of God. 2. One that excites admiration or awe.
— WEBSTER'S II NEW RIVERSIDE DICTIONARY

TODAY, HEAVEN IS all around us—or the symbols of heaven, at least. Walk down any avenue, through any museum, by any store window and you'll see them. Puffy white clouds painted on wallpaper and pillowcases, moon-shaped crystals and sunbeams adorning cards and stationery, rainbows splashed across everything from bedspreads to Beanie Babies. Stars of every shape and color decorate dishware and dangle from necklaces and earrings. And who hasn't seen a child's bedroom dotted with clusters of glow-in-the-dark stars and planets, whose soft light lulls toddlers to sleep and stirs the imagination and dreams of ten-year-old boys and girls?

Even more prevalent than sunbeams and moonbeams in today's world are heavenly angels. There are angel books and angel calendars. Angel imagery is etched on jewelry, expensive artwork, pottery, and sculpture. Winged cherubs decorate coffee tables and mantelpieces in homes that, a few years ago, never had a hint of an angel except, perhaps, in December atop a Christmas tree. Why this resurgence in angel awareness? Why the sudden prevalence of books, movies, and television shows about heaven, angels, and miracles?

After talking to hundreds of people in the past few years about their experiences with miracles, we have witnessed firsthand the kind of spiritual awakening reported by so many as we approached the dawn of a new millennium. The stars and angels around us symbolically tell of a people in search of something beyond this life, a hope for an existence more peaceful than that of the frightened and weary world in which they live. In the midst of everyday stress and struggle, we want to believe and be reassured that there is a greater purpose to our lives.

At times, we even feel a certain emptiness, a longing for something beyond the day-to-day unfolding of our lives. It may almost feel like homesickness—a yearning for another time and place we once might have called home, or might, in the distant future. A warm and wonderful place where there's no loneliness or sorrow and where only love abounds. Logically we can't quite grasp it, but our hearts tell us this feeling has something to do with that place we call heaven. Perhaps, as we continue the inner search for peace and serenity, our soul cries out, "Where on earth can I find heaven?"

Some have found it. Many, in fact, have. What we've discovered in our extensive "miracle quest" is that these glorious glimpses of heaven are like precious gifts given to very ordinary people all over the world. It's not that God grants miracles willy-nilly. Certainly not on demand. But miracles come more often than we might suppose, and it's very likely that every family has at least one story they could tell. Each small miracle seems to come as part of a greater plan, to accomplish a thing of worth, to help change a life, in addition to offering comfort. Heavenly miracles—proof of God's love and involvement in our lives—are all around us.

Some miracles are so private and sacred that they are not meant to be shared but to be savored quietly in moments of reflection and prayer. Others are so transforming that they must be told. The miracles in this book are messages from heaven that beg to be passed on, for they contain important lessons for us all. You will be moved by the story of a woman who mysteriously appears to lead a young boy across the mine-infested German-Austrian border to find his family; the story of a little girl whose life is immeasurably enriched by visits from the grandfather who died years before she was born; the account of a man who spots a Bible engraved with a name that leads him to his long-lost father; and the heart-warming tale of a man and a woman brought together in love through identical words revealed to both in separate dreams. Each of these soul-stretching experiences becomes a turning point, a reminder that the hand of God is always there, guiding us through our days.

Heavenly miracles by their very nature often speak of connections to loved ones who have passed away. "Each departed friend," wrote one observer, "is a magnet that attracts us to the next world." Many of these stories point to the extraordinary bond that exists between mother and son, grandmother and granddaughter, or husband and wife, in life as well as in death. And with each account, we are amazed and inspired by the enduring power of love and the eternal strength of family.

But life doesn't always present a perfectly tidy picture. There is pain, sickness, tragedy, and loss, to be sure. Suffering forces our attention toward places we would normally neglect, and it is during life's stormy seasons, it would seem, that the miracles rush in. It is when we arrive at that difficult point where we don't know what more we can do that God steps in and takes us by the hand. It is at that precise moment—when He finally has our attention—that we are allowed a glimpse of the wonders heaven holds for us. There may be unanswered questions still, but we know that He loves us, and knowing that, for the moment, is enough.

"The soul would have no rainbow if the eyes had no tears," the old proverb says. Certainly, many of the events in these stories were cause for sadness and tears at the time, but for the people whose lives were touched by miracles, the tears were only a prelude to hope and joy. It is our hope that the remarkable stories in *Heavenly Miracles* will fill your heart with peace and enrich your soul with all the hues of heaven's most splendid rainbow.

JAMIE
LAURA
JENNIFER

A Path Through the Wilderness

I WAS TEN YEARS old in June of 1941, when the German Army invaded the Carpatho-Ukraine where I lived with my parents and four younger brothers and sisters. All of the able-bodied men, including my father, were rounded up to be sent to the Balkans, where they were placed in forced labor camps.

Over the next three years my mother, Margaret Kozauer, took her five children daily into the fields. From sunrise to sunset we worked in order to raise enough food to try to keep us all alive.

In October of 1944, the German Army came to our village again, pushed back by Stalin's Red Army. Women and children were given two hours to pack our personal belongings to prepare for evacuation. Then we were transported by train to a refugee camp in Silesia, Poland. The daily rations of food were so inadequate that soon many of the very old and very young began to die. My baby sister, Cecilia, died of starvation.

Along with all boys over the age of eight, I was soon sent to a Nazi youth camp in the Austrian Alps near Salzburg, to be taught German and Nazi philosophy. Life in this camp was extremely harsh, involving both physical and mental cruelty.

When the war in Europe ended on May 8, 1945, the Nazi personnel and guards in the camp disappeared abruptly, leaving a camp full of frightened young boys alone to fend for ourselves. What should I do? Where should I go? Was anyone in my family still alive?

Not knowing the answers, I went to the Salzburg rail station and climbed onto a parked freight train carrying horses and straw. During the night the train slowly began to move; I had no idea where it was going. It took me to Nuremberg, Germany.

Postwar Germany was teeming with over ten million refugees, all trying to locate family members. From May until September, I rode freight trains from camp to camp, sleeping at night on park benches, living on handouts or fruit stolen from trees. Due to the poor diet and unsanitary life, my skin was covered with rashes, my gums were bleeding, and my hands constantly shook. I knew I would not survive the coming winter if I didn't find suitable shelter soon.

It was the third week in September when I got off a train in Bamberg and was stopped by two Silesian nuns. When they heard my story, they invited me to their convent, where they offered me a bowl of warm soup. It was the first real meal I had had in months. My hands were trembling so badly that each spoonful of soup would spill before reaching my mouth.

The nuns had to improvise for me, pouring the soup into a mug so I could grasp it with two hands and drink.

The nuns told me that this was a convent for girls only, but they knew where I would be safe—the Carmelite Monastery on the other side of town. There I was given medical care, three meals a day, and best of all, a warm, safe place to sleep.

In an effort to reunite families who had been separated by the war, city newspapers would publish lists of names of refugees and their locations. The monastery sent in my name—Nikolaus Kozauer—to be listed. I prayed that my mother was still alive and would somehow find me. Weeks became months, and I received no news. I felt terribly alone in this war-ravaged world.

But my prayers were finally answered in early December. One day I looked up to see my mother standing before me. Someone had spotted my name in the Munich newspaper and given my mother the information. To come and find me, she had to leave my brothers—seven-year-old John and five-year-old Thomas, with my ten-year-old sister Agnes in charge. Worried about their safety, she hoped to make the trip from Austria to Germany and back as quickly as possible.

It was wonderful to be with Mother again, but our struggle wasn't over. I needed papers in order to return to Austria, and the authorities told us it would take about three weeks to obtain clearance to cross the border. How could my mother leave her other young children alone for three long weeks? She was determined not to leave without me, but three weeks was too long to wait. We realized we would have to sneak across the border.

We would have to traverse a dense and unfamiliar forest,

walking first to the west and then turning south, to reach the freedom that awaited us in Austria. With no one to guide us through these bewildering surroundings, my mother's determination to reunite her family prompted her to turn to the only source of comfort she knew—prayer.

In the deep, winter chill of that December night, guided only by the moonlight, my mother held my cold hand as she prayed the Rosary over and over, putting her faith in the Virgin Mary's protection.

Then, out of nowhere, a woman in a long dress appeared. Fixing us with a solemn gaze, she said simply, "Follow me." In silence she led us south through the woods in a zigzag route for about twenty-five minutes. We were too stunned and too grateful to ask any questions; we just instinctively trusted her. Suddenly she stopped and pointed ahead. In the distance, we could just make out a glimmer of lights. It was an Austrian city. Our hearts leaped at the sight of home. Still holding hands, my mother and I turned to thank our silent guide, but she had disappeared. Where had she gone? Was it possible that a desperate mother's prayer had been answered by some divine miracle?

We learned later that the Austrian-German border that we had crossed that night was heavily infested with minefields. The zigzag path that we followed through those dark woods with the assistance of the mysterious woman had been the only safe route. We never would've found it on our own.

Believing that Our Blessed Mother had answered her desperate prayers, my mother dedicated her life to the daily recitation of the Rosary. Until the day she died in 1996, she always ended her prayers with, "Holy Mary, mother of God, thank you for helping and protecting my children and me, Amen."

Nikolaus Kozauer, Ph.D.
Toms River, New Jersey

Silvery Moon

OR AS LONG AS I can remember, my grand-mother and I were the best of friends. One of the things we liked best was talking for hours in her farm-house kitchen. She'd bake chocolate brownies with wal-nuts—my favorite—and we'd sit there eating and talking about everything and nothing. I remember one afternoon in particular when I was a grown woman. It would have been completely perfect, except that we both knew she was slowly dying of cancer. She asked me that day, out of the blue, if I recalled a time when I was just a little girl and she and I had looked at the moon together. "Do you remember how sad you were that Gramp and I had to go back to Massachusetts the next day?" It seemed really important to her that I remember. A fuzzy picture filled my mind.

"Sort of. I think so . . . ," I replied, struggling to bring the memory into focus.

She sighed and got a faraway, dreamy look in her eyes. "You know, I'll never forget that night. You got so excited when I explained that I could see the same moon in Massachusetts that you could see in Virginia. It made you feel so much better. And ever since then I've always thought of you every time I look at the moon. We made a deal, you and I, remember?"

The picture in my mind became a little less blurry. "Were we drinking grape juice?" I asked.

"Yes," Gram said, smiling and nodding her head slowly, savoring the memory. "We were." And suddenly I remembered perfectly.

I was four years old. My family and I lived in Virginia. Because of the distance, we didn't see my grandparents more than once or twice a year. To a young child, it felt like a lifetime between visits. I was always thrilled when Gram and Gramp came to visit and then completely devastated—the way only little children can be devastated—each time they had to leave. The night before one visit's end my grandmother and I went outside to sit on the apartment stoop, drink grape juice, and look at the stars. It was a beautiful, warm night, filled with the sound of crickets, and washed with the blue light of the moon. I sipped sweet purple grape juice from a tall Tupperware cup. The chewed-up rim felt rough on my lips. I leaned into my grandmother's body and she put her arm around my shoulders. She knew I was sad.

"Hey!" she said, trying to cheer me up, "see the moon up there?" I nodded dully, not interested in being cheered. Gram continued undaunted: "Well, did you know that that is the very same moon that is shining over Massachusetts right now, over our house, over the whole farm? I could be looking at that same moon right now, if I were there."

I sat up and looked above us, a little more interested. "Are you sure it's the *same* moon?" I asked, skeptically. She assured me that it was. The thought that we could both see the same thing at the same time, even if we were far apart, was an exciting and novel concept.

"You know what?" she said. "When I go home, I'll look at the moon in Massachusetts and you can look at it down here. I'll think about you, and you can think about me and it will almost be like we're together. We'll be doing the same thing at the same time. It can be our little secret. We'll think of each other whenever we see the moon, okay?"

It was a deal. I looked at the moon and thought about her a lot when I was young. It made me feel so much closer to her, knowing she might be doing the same thing: looking at the moon and thinking about me.

And then, I guess because I got older, I forgot about "our moon"—until that particular afternoon when she asked me if I remembered, and it all came back to me in such vivid detail. My grandmother had given me the gift of connection to her not only when I was a lonely four-year-old, but once again when I was a grown and married woman facing the loss of someone I dearly loved.

It wasn't long afterward that my grandmother passed away. It was my first experience with death. When she died, we were living several hundred miles apart. I felt so empty inside, as if someone had reached in and ripped out a big chunk of me. I felt so far away from her, like somehow, impossibly, she was truly gone forever. My greatest fear was that I would go back to Massachusetts for her funeral and find the same emptiness there. I was terrified that I would find her gone from the places we'd loved together. Afraid that I would find her gone from my heart, even in all the places that had been so special to us. "Please God, please," I prayed. "I know you've taken her to be home with you, but please help me stop feeling so empty. I just want a small piece of her back to fill this hole in my heart."

It poured rain the entire trip back to Massachusetts. For seven hours I watched the rain beat against the windshield. The swish of the wipers sounded tauntingly like "She's gone. She's gone. She's gone," over and over again.

When we finally arrived, despite the darkness and the rain, I needed to get out of the car and walk. My fear was suffocating and I had to face it. I knew I needed to stop covering my heart. I needed to peek through, like a frightened child facing a monster, and just accept what I saw.

And incredibly, what I saw as I stood in a field of rain-wet grass, took a deep breath and opened my eyes, was a clear September sky and the breathtaking face of a full moon. I was finally ready to accept the emptiness, but instead, there was a full moon to fill my heart with its pale, silvery light. Once again, my grandmother had reached out across the distance from wherever she was, to reassure a scared and lonely girl that she was still very much a part of that girl's life.

KAREN C. DRISCOLL
Frederick, Maryland

Matchmaker in Heaven

ARGE BLOND WOMAN enjoys walks on the beach, quiet candlelit dinners, and romance." It was a good ad and it drew lots of response. The only thing was, I didn't write it.

In 1973 I was working as a live-in nurse's aide at a home for the aged. My boss, Doris, was always urging me to date, saying I was a pretty woman with a lot of love to offer. Well, she was partially right—I was full of love and I enjoyed taking care of my patients, but I also wasn't ready for a serious relationship.

One night in March of that year, I had a strange dream of a beautiful woman with long red hair sitting at a church organ. She turned to me and said that I should write an ad as worded above, and send it to a certain newspaper. When I awoke, I wrote the words down and left the paper by my bed.

When Doris came into the room she found the paper and

asked about it. I told her it was just some nonsense from a dream I had had, and to pay no attention to it. Three days later, however, I had another dream of the woman with the red hair. This time she said very plainly, "Respond only to the typewritten letter." I had no idea what she meant. When I finally confided in Doris, she laughed and then sheepishly admitted that she had sent my ad to the newspaper because she wanted so badly for me to find a mate.

I should've been angry at Doris, but instead I felt strangely excited as I waited to see if my ad drew a response. I began to wonder if some of the things told to me by my Apache Indian grandmother, with whom I had grown up, might actually be coming true.

"The Spirit will bring you a mate because you are so special," she would tell me over and over again.

Trusting her wisdom but being too young to fully understand, I would ask, "But what do you mean by 'special'?"

"Oh, my child," she'd say, "you have a very special gift—a way of seeing things before they happen. Even if you choose not to listen to your dreams, somehow the Spirit will guide you and bring about good things in your life."

Two weeks after my strange dreams I received a large envelope in the mail. Inside were more than sixty-five letters—responses to the ad Doris had placed. I quickly thumbed through them and, to my astonishment, found only one that was typewritten. It read in part, "Hello, my name is Jim Kelly. I too would like quiet walks on the beach, although it has been quite a while since I have been in a relationship."

I called him right away, and his voice was as I dreamed it would be—soft, smooth, and full of caring. He described himself to me: five foot nine with reddish brown hair, a power-weight lifter, an ex-law officer who now worked in a security business. At first I was hesitant to tell him much about myself. Then I had a vision of my grandmother's face encouraging me, and I slowly shared some things about myself.

I didn't want to meet Jim right away, but Doris told me she'd fire me if I didn't go out with him, so I arranged a date. We met at a dance. For me, it was love at first sight. Jim was handsome with soft brown eyes. We danced throughout the night and he told me how beautiful I was. A perfect gentleman, he was very attentive and considerate of me. Several times, I had to hold back tears of gratitude that we had been brought together. It felt so right.

Our relationship evolved quickly and we grew to love each other deeply. One night, we were looking through some of Jim's old picture albums. As I turned a page, one of the pictures startled me. It was a photograph of a woman with red hair. She was sitting at an organ, just like the woman who had appeared in my dream. When I asked Jim about the picture, his eyes filled with tears. He said that the woman in the photograph was his late wife, Georgia, who had died of cancer several years earlier. Although Jim had told me about losing his wife and had always spoken of her with great love, I had never known what she looked like or that she had played the organ for churches in the surrounding community.

As Jim and I continued to share our thoughts and feelings, he confided that he, too, had dreamed that he should answer an ad like the one I had written. I told him about my grandmother and her belief that I would be led to certain good things in my life, and that it was my faith in her that had prompted me to call him and have the courage to keep our first date.

It has been more than twenty-five years since the night we met, and I have never known anything but love and devotion from Jim. He is not only my husband and my lover, but he is also my best friend, and I feel like the luckiest woman in the world to have been led to him. We have even gone into the ministry together, trying to help other married couples work through their differences and come to understand how love can grow and be sustained.

But I have developed another deep friendship over the years. Georgia, the beautiful woman with the long red hair who came to me in my dreams so many years ago, has been there for me in spirit, and I believe has helped me be the best possible wife and companion to Jim. We include her in our lives, placing flowers at her grave on special holidays and on her birthday, and we talk often about her and how grateful we are for the blessing she has been in our lives. One thing is certain: love must be Georgia's watchword, for she brought about a most incredible miracle that made it possible for Jim and me to discover exactly that.

KRIS KELLY
St. Petersburg, Florida

Helen's Gift

AS CHRISTMAS APPROACHED, my children, Roger, David, and Ellie, and I began decorating our home with greens and sparkly tinsel, glittered pinecones, and shiny gold ribbon. Our holiday decorations looked different this year, though: they were somewhat sparse and definitely less commercial. When I had divorced several years before, I had sent the elegant nativity set and most of the Christmas ornaments with my ex-husband. That was fine with me; they belonged to his childhood and I had little attachment to them. But now, a refined traditional touch was missing from our Christmas.

I carefully pulled the packing straw off the homemade nativity scene I had made when the children were little. In my own childhood, my mother had called our nativity scene a *crèche*, a French word for *cradle* or *nativity*, and the one I had made for my children was crafted from wood turnings I found at the hardware store in rural Nevada where we lived. On some, I had painted beards, headdresses, and long robes to make them look like shepherds and wise men. I used a small wooden egg to represent the baby Jesus, a larger wooden pear for Mary, and wooden Tinkertoys for the simple stable.

It worked well because the children could handle (and drop) the unbreakable figures as they played out the Christmas story. I have sweet memories of chocolate fingerprints on a wise man, and of the baby Jesus clutched tightly in chubby little fists. As the children grew older, the crèche had sentimental value, but we all yearned for one that had a little more dignity. Each year, as we unpacked the Christmas things, someone predictably said, "When are we going to get a new crèche?"

Year after year I searched the stores to find one that was just right. I looked at nativity sets from all over the world made from every conceivable material, representing every imaginable interpretation of that historic night. Most of the characters looked stern or pompous, or so cute that they trivialized the holiness surrounding the birth of Christ.

Then last Christmas season, while buying a gift at a department store, I glanced above the register at a little figure on the back counter—a small clay donkey lying on its side with a broken leg. I moved around to look closely and felt drawn to his gentle little face. When I asked if he belonged to a nativity set, the clerk showed me the other pieces, each one delightful and beautifully handcrafted out of clay with stiffened fabric clothes and hand-painted faces. I knew the minute I saw them that we had found our crèche at last.

The price matched the quality of the workmanship, however, and I wasn't sure it was a wise purchase for me. Nonetheless, when the clerk offered to order an unbroken set for me from another store, I agreed, figuring I could decide in the meantime. Amid the commercial blitz that Christmas had become, I somehow wanted to add the holiness of the nativity story to our home.

The week passed and the store called to notify me that the crèche had arrived. I promised to pick it up in the next three days. Five days went by, but I couldn't make up my mind. One day I wholeheartedly embraced its purchase; the next day I panicked at the expense.

The store called again. I had to decide. Still ambivalent, I called every three days for two weeks to renew the "hold" on the crèche just one more time. Finally I decided to leave it up to fate. I was leaving town for a weekend wedding; if the set was unsold when I returned, I'd buy it. If it sold, I'd do without.

When I returned Sunday night, the message on the answering machine reported that a woman desperately wanted the crèche; if the store didn't hear from me, the crèche would be sold to her. The message had been left on Saturday and I hadn't heard it until late Sunday night. My heart sank. I knew it was too late. Fate indeed had intervened! The nativity set had probably been sold and would be part of someone else's memories now. Just as well, I thought. But I still mourned the beautiful scene.

On Monday morning I dragged myself to the mailbox to get the accumulated mail. Tucked among the glaring ads and giant foil-lined Christmas card envelopes was a humble little white envelope. It was the one I always looked forward to receiving during the holiday season—the only one ever addressed in ink from a fountain pen.

The ritual was the same every year. After carefully opening the envelope I would pull out the cherished little card. No glitzy, funky Santa jokes in Day-Glo or snowy pine trees in a clichéd scene. The card, a breath of childlike innocence, offered a nativity scene, simply drawn and colored in soft pastel shades. Inside was the guileless message in the familiar script of Cousin Helen.

Helen should have been called a great aunt instead of cousin. In her late eighties now, she was my beloved grandmother's cousin, the last of her generation in our family. Her life had been devoted to teaching kindergarten in Wisconsin, with her summers spent at a lake that I remembered as a magical and happy place.

I met her once when I was seven and then again when I was thirteen. Since we lived in California, we never saw her again. But every Christmas Cousin Helen sent me a little check, usually for five dollars, with a sweet note telling me about her travels and life up at the lake. She always said, "Get a little something for yourself." I wrote her thank-you notes and occasionally chatty letters about me and some of the family news.

As I got older, she sent ten dollars. I loved receiving the money, but I loved even more the unpretentious cards and the gentle personal notes complimenting me on my writing and my activities. When I married and had a family, the checks got larger to accommodate the numbers, with a note designating the money for the children and always "a little something for yourself." After I divorced, I used her checks to restore our Christmas decorations, buying each child a special ornament to take with them and enjoy when they had their own families. Over the years our tree, mantel, and table sparkled with Cousin Helen's generosity.

Now, standing on the front steps, I plucked the little envelope from the stack and sat down to savor the message. Always before reading the note, my eyes fondly scanned the perfect loops of the ys and ps, the evenly crossed ts, indicative of her career as a teacher. The card was the same angelic scene, but this time the handwriting was different—it was shaky, and the message was brief.

After forty years of opening her cards and reading Cousin Helen's news of the midwestern winters and her travels to Florida, I knew something was different this time. My stomach felt heavy. The message told of her ill health and apologized for the brevity of the note. As always, she wished the "darling children a wonderful Christmas," and again, told me to get "a little something for yourself."

Tears blurred her affectionate signature. My heart began to ache. I had never thought of Cousin Helen as getting older. While she'd always been "older," neither the cards nor the handwriting had ever changed in all the years I'd received them. I'd always thought of myself as the eternal little girl writing to a favorite cousin by the lake. Now, suddenly, Cousin Helen was old, and with it, frail. At the bottom she had added an afterthought. I wept as I read it: "Thank you, dear, for all the wonderful letters and pictures you've sent throughout the years. They have meant so much to me." I was surprised to realize how much a part of my life she was, how close we were, how familiar. Forty years of little notes.

As I dropped the letter, the check fell in my lap. The amount was larger than ever before. Almost three times more than before! The amount, in fact, was exactly the price of the crèche. Oh yes, this was the perfect gift from Cousin Helen. What greater legacy could she leave than the spirit of Christmas so lovingly and beautifully displayed, a timeless remembrance of our enduring friendship.

I dashed to the phone and dialed from memory the store's number. No, the clerk said, the nativity set hadn't been sold. It still had my name on it. Miracle! Within minutes I raced to the store and bought the crèche, my heart overflowing as Christmas carols played joyfully around me.

That night, my children and I gathered around our bare table, which stood in the soft glow of the Christmas tree lights. One by one, each little box was unwrapped, tissue gently pulled from each figure's face. Each one came with a note explaining its name and character and its personal view of how that momentous night might have been experienced. Each child waited his turn, listening to the others read, and then carefully added his piece to the scene on the table.

Then we stood back and looked. The awe of that holy night of long ago filled our hearts as we gazed at each figure, the fabric robes and hats carefully draped and tucked around clay faces and hands. The expressions were gentle and wise, gazing in awe as the babe in the manger innocently lay at his adoring mother's side.

I felt warm all over, marveling at the power of love brought into this world along with the admonition to share it. I thought of the tender feelings I shared with Cousin Helen, whom I had seen only twice in forty years but with whom I shared such a timeless bond. And now, as we pull out the big crèche box each year and ceremoniously unwrap each figure, we think of that gift of love from above as well as the one so humbly shared by Cousin Helen as just "a little something for yourself."

HILARY HINKLEY
Sacramento, California

Flight of an Eagle

*E*LIJAH WAS THE kind of kid who drove you crazy, but you had to love him anyway. He had an exceptional way of viewing the world, one that made you realize he was way ahead of the rest in his ability to understand the important things in life. And now, a few short weeks away from his eighth birthday, he was excited about the upcoming event that would officially make him truly belong in his family once and for all—the finalization of the adoption that had been so agonizingly long in the making.

Eli was looking forward to changing not only his last name for good, but his middle name as well. He had decided that his name should be changed to Elijah Makana "Golden Eagle." It was an unusual name, but no one could talk him out of it. His mom and dad had chosen "Makana" because it meant "gift" in Hawaiian, which was most certainly what Eli had been to them. But "Golden Eagle" was Eli's choice, and the name he was most adamant about. Ever since his dad had gone to Alaska and brought back a T-shirt with a golden eagle on it, the great bird had become Eli's symbol and his passion. Just about anyone who came in contact with him knew of his love for eagles. In fact, his collection of eagle paraphernalia was known for miles around. His parents had agreed that "Golden Eagle" should become a part of his legal name once the adoption was final.

Elijah had been a part of my life for almost four years. Shortly after he came to live with his new family, his mother, a friend of mine, asked if I would take him to church with me. She didn't feel ready to start attending church herself, but she wanted Eli to go. And so, week after week, this exuberant little boy wormed his way into my heart. At first Eli didn't know how to act in church and spent most of the time rolling around on the floor or kicking the seat in front of him or asking (loudly) what we were doing after church. As time went on, however, he became a model churchgoer and participated in all the activities. He worked his charm on the other members and quickly became an integral part of the Children's Church. And each Sunday he'd spend the afternoon at my house while his mom was working. He even started calling me "Grandma" just like all my other grandchildren, and was as much a part of the family as the rest of them.

There was something special about Eli. As he matured in his thinking, he often asked questions about God and Jesus and other things like baptism and communion. When he sought out the pastor or one of the elders for prayer, his depth of understanding surprised me. His church teachers said he was usually first to volunteer to lead the group in songs and prayers, and he often talked with other church members about his upcoming adoption and how much it meant to him.

But the adoption never took place.

One night in the middle of November, Eli and his mom were getting ready to go to a Cub Scout meeting. While she was getting dressed, she reminded Eli, "Now don't get your uniform dirty while you're waiting for me. I'll be ready in a few minutes and then we'll stop at the store and pick up some treats to share at the meeting."

"I'm just going to look for my Scout book," Eli shouted, racing out the door, "and, Mom, can we bring pretzels to the meeting this time?"

When Eli's mother headed out to the car about fifteen minutes later, Eli was nowhere to be found. She wasn't terribly concerned, however, because they had a big yard that a boy could easily lose himself in. The closest source of any real danger was a busy highway almost two miles away, so it wasn't until his parents had searched for Eli for several minutes throughout the yard that they started to worry. Their search finally ended, tragically, on the busy highway. By the time they arrived, a crowd had gathered around the little boy who had been hit by a car. Dressed in a Cub Scout uniform, he was still clutching a book tightly in his hand.

As I stood by his battered body in the hospital emergency room alongside his mom and dad, I prayed that he would live, although I couldn't imagine how he would ever survive the trauma he had endured. I think I knew deep down that Eli wouldn't be spending any more Sunday afternoons with me, but despite my sadness I was somehow overcome with great peace about where he would be instead.

Only God and Eli knew what made him go up to the high-way that day and how he got there so quickly. Was he just eager to get going and tired of waiting for his mother? Was he afraid the store would run out of pretzels before they could get there? Did he run up there? Did someone give him a ride?

Eli never regained consciousness and was pronounced dead the next day after having been air-evacuated to a hospital in Honolulu. He had been kept on life support all night, but his dad said he felt certain that Eli had actually left his body somewhere in midair between our island, Hawaii, and Oahu. Somewhere a Golden Eagle might take flight.

Even in their grief at losing this precious child, his parents unselfishly donated his organs. Several undamaged organs—a kidney, liver, corneas, heart valves—went to give life and sight to several other people, including a two-year-old girl whose body had just rejected another donor's liver just days before it accepted Eli's. These were lasting gifts of love from Eli, and from his devoted parents.

A memorial service for Eli was held on November 30, 1998. It would have been his eighth birthday. It was the birthday he had dreamed of for so long—the day when he'd officially receive his new name. A birthday party "with lots of people" was what he had requested, and "lots of balloons."

Eli got both his wishes that day as over three hundred people gathered for a celebration of his life, complete with birthday cake and balloons. Hundreds of helium balloons were released in honor of Eli's lofty hopes and dreams, his goodness, and his faith in God.

As the colored balloons slowly rose into the sky, they drifted toward the family's home. Then someone in the group pointed and remarked that one of the white balloons seemed to be leading the way. One by one, heads turned heavenward, and then people started to gasp at what they saw. There was no doubt about it. A group of blue balloons follwed the white one as they began to spread out and form something recognizable. Against the soft colors of an afternoon sky, the balloons had taken the shape of an eagle in full flight.

As much as he wanted it, Eli never legally got his parents' last name. But all who were there that afternoon knew without a doubt that Eli would always carry his self-appointed middle name with him, as God welcomed a young but very majestic "Golden Eagle" into heaven.

SHELLEY L. BEREMAN-BENEVIDES
Hilo, Hawaii

A Pope's Blessing

HOUSEHOLD ACCIDENT IS every mother's greatest fear. Small children move so quickly, faster than our watchful eyes can anticipate. On the fateful day that my baby moved faster than I did, I was thankful that God—and one of His most holy saints—were there to protect little Eileen.

It was almost Christmas in 1973 and I was working at a seasonal job selling toys for a toy company. It required my being out of the house only a few hours a week, and during the time I was away, my husband could supervise the kids' homework and bedtime routines. With seven young children, we were grateful for the extra money, which helped pay household (and Santa's) expenses.

The owner of the toy company had visited Rome earlier that year and had brought back religious medals for all of her employees. Each medal held a relic of Pope John XXIII.

Being Catholic myself, I admired Pope John for his gentle nature and lively sense of humor. I promptly mailed a brief thank-you note to my employer and life continued at its busy preholiday pace. My baby, Eileen, was two years old at the time and was a typical toddler—inquisitive, active, climbing everywhere, and getting into everything. I was standing just a few feet away from her in my kitchen when the events unfolded that still cause me to marvel all these years later.

My new medal of Pope John had been sitting on the kitchen counter for a day or two, and I decided to slip it onto my key ring. The door key was on one end of the key ring, and since there was an empty ring on the other end, I attached the medal there, and then left the whole thing on the counter. No sooner had I done so than little Eileen climbed onto the kitchen stool and with amazing speed, grabbed it off the counter. Harmless enough—a child playing with a set of keys—but to be on the safe side, I reached out to take them from her. Before I could stop her, she turned and inserted the key into an electric outlet on the control panel of my electric range.

I watched in horror as she jolted through the air and was thrown to the floor. The power in the house went out amid flying sparks. Frantic, I scooped my baby into my arms. Praying as I held her to me, I looked down and saw that her tiny hand was completely black. An electrical burn? I was horrified. But no, her hand was covered with soot that brushed right off.

I was astounded when I realized that Eileen actually seemed to be unharmed. Comforting her as she sobbed and thanking God at the same time, I picked up the key ring, which lay on the metal top of the stove. The key itself was very hot to the touch. To my amazement, the image of Pope John's face was scarred where the medal had touched metal and melted. I was mystified. With such a powerful jolt of electricity, how was it possible that Eileen was unharmed? Suddenly I understood: because the pope's medal dangled from the opposite end of the key ring, it had touched the top of the stove and grounded it, completing the current of electricity. If only the key had been on the ring, as it had been just moments before the incident, the charge would have been enough to do serious and permanent damage to my baby. My heart told me that angels and saints can intervene with nature in miraculous ways.

Many years have passed, and Eileen is now a college graduate. The medal with the scarred likeness of Pope John XXIII is with me always and means even more to me now than it did years ago. Each time I look at the medal I think about God and His chosen helpers—those who inspire us, guide us, and protect us, and sometimes even bear our burdens and take on the scars of our human frailties. The medal is a constant reminder that not all miracles are grand, public events that make the news. As I show people the scars on the face of Pope John, I explain that miracles and blessings come in all sizes and can happen to anyone, anywhere . . . even in a humble kitchen.

MARIE FOLEY NIELSEN
Toms River, New Jersey

An Angel's Hand

OUR OLDEST DAUGHTER, Kathleen, was nearly sixteen. She was too young to seriously date, her father and I had decided, but she had a boyfriend. One evening, when I was leaving to pick up our son, Paul, from baseball practice, she asked if she could go with her boyfriend to pick up his younger brother at a friend's house.

"All right. Just make sure you wear your seat belts, and come right home," I cautioned. It was my father's birthday, and our youngest daughter, Therese, was already at my parents' house waiting for us to arrive with the cake I had yet to pick up at the store.

I drove to the school to pick up Paul, deciding to take the highway, rather than the usual shortcut along the back roads. Then we drove to the store for the cake and a few last-minute goodies. As we left the parking lot, we suddenly saw a parade of paramedics, fire trucks, three ambulances, and a multitude of police cars, all responding to a call.

I had a sick feeling in my stomach and said to Paul, "Somebody needs our prayers, quick." I wondered if it was a fire or a bad car accident. At one of the intersections I had to stop to let still more emergency vehicles through, and I began to pray.

"Lord, those people need you right now. Go to them and place your protective hand over them. Let guardian angels help them, make them safe, keep them from harm."

We stopped at my parents' to drop off the food before going home to pick up Kathleen. My father met me at the car.

"Which way did you go to the school?" he asked. "There was a bad accident on the back road and I heard someone was killed. It happened just about the time you had to pick up Paul, and I know you always go that way. I was so relieved to see you pull in because I had a terrible gut feeling it might have been you, Barbara."

Paul and I drove the short distance home. As we approached our driveway, I could see that our house was dark. That was strange, because whenever Kathleen was home alone, she always turned on every light. As I turned off the ignition, tears began to fall unbidden. "It was Kathleen," I told Paul, "I know it."

I ran into the house and checked our answering machine. No one had called. I let out a sigh of relief, thinking that there would be a message by now if something were wrong. But then the phone rang. It was the mother of one of Kathleen's friends who worked in the local hospital emergency room.

"Before I tell you anything, I want you to calm down," she began. I wouldn't let her finish. "I know, there was an accident," I stated flatly, numbness setting in. "How is Kathleen?"

"Just bring someone with you," she encouraged. My heart sank.

I didn't call my husband at work, nor my parents. Paul and I just left for the hospital immediately. As I pulled into the parking lot, one of the paramedics, someone we have known for years, met us outside.

"I'm sorry, I'm so sorry," he said, tears streaming down his face. "In all of my years as a paramedic I have never seen a car wrecked so badly. It was split in half. I'm so sorry!"

The next thing I remember, I was speaking to the doctor in the hallway of the ER. The first thing he did was to ask me if I believed in God. My knees gave way. "No," he said, "you don't understand. Do you believe in divine intervention?"

I stammered a weak yes. "Someone was watching over those kids tonight," the doctor said. "It was truly a miracle that no one was killed or seriously injured." He smiled and asked me tenderly, "Do you know what shirt your daughter is wearing tonight?"

I shook my head, and he told me to go down the hall and look. But before I did, he said emphatically, "Your daughter is blessed with angels and so are you. From what the emergency personnel told me, there is no way that your daughter should be alive, let alone have only a few scratches."

I found Kathleen lying on a gurney, waiting for more X rays. I reached out to her, and we both started sobbing. I couldn't believe she was alive and well enough to be talking and crying with me. In a few hours, all three children were treated and released with only minor scrapes and bruises. On the way home that night, Kathleen told me this story:

"It was really weird. About a quarter of a mile before the accident, I said, 'Wait, we forgot to put our seat belts on. My mother will kill me.' Suddenly, a car came barreling toward us in our lane. He swerved and I knew we got hit at full impact on the passenger side of the car—right where I was sitting. He hit us three times because the car kept spinning in circles. I felt the hand of my boyfriend's little brother on my shoulder from the backseat, holding me tightly in place. Even after it was all over and the car had stopped spinning, I could still feel his hand on my shoulder. But when I looked around, I saw that he had been thrown out the back window of the car!

"It was an angel, Mom, I know it!"

The next day we went to look at the car. I felt sick when I saw it. Unbelievably, it had been split in half, right underneath my daughter's seat. There was no way Kathleen should have lived through this terrible crash. The driver of the other car, who we later found out was driving with a suspended license, was traveling ninety to ninety-five miles per hour, according to witnesses. The point of impact at that deadly speed was directly at Kathleen's door. The police report stated that the car door was found fifty feet away from the accident scene, with the seat belt attached. So when the door broke loose, Kathleen had no seat belt to hold her down. The "hand" was the only thing that saved my daughter's life.

We were truly humbled by God's love, the power of prayer, and the helping hand of guardian angels. The Lord had known, long before I did, that my child was in trouble. I will always praise Him for saving her life and restoring faith to mine. When I prayed for Him to protect the "somebody" who needed help, it had already been done.

Kathleen is a grown woman now with a child of her own. I am sure that in the years to come as she watches her son grow, she'll have moments of concern for his safety when she'll call upon a guardian angel, as I called upon mine. After her experience with the protective hand that saved her life, she has no doubt that God and His angels are very real—here to help us in times of need.

There's one more thing. After I embraced Kathleen when she was lying on the hospital gurney, I remembered the doctor telling me to look at the shirt she was wearing. I glanced down and, at first, thought it was just another one of her plain white T-shirts, but I was astounded when I saw what the doctor was talking about. There, across the front of her shirt in bold letters were the words JESUS SAVES.

BARBARA PITCAVAGE
Swoyersville, Pennsylvania

Thanks, Dad

MY DAUGHTER, CHRISTINA, and my father have a loving but unusual relationship. They talk in hushed whispers late at night, he reads her stories when she can't sleep, and he has, on occasion, placed toys and stuffed animals in her bed to comfort her when she's sick. He goes to her room when she is frightened at night and sings to her so that my wife and I can sleep. Christina tells us about her games with her grandpa and keeps our whole family informed about the details of their talks.

The most wonderful thing about my father's love for his granddaughter is its capacity to span time and heaven. You see, my father passed away six years before my wife and I met—obviously before Christina was even born.

Christina is only two years old. For most people, the mere mention of that age flips the switch of a mental neon sign, blinking TERRIBLE TWOS!, bringing images of temper tantrums in restaurants, screaming fits in the checkout line, or parental mad dashes across parking lots—abandoning grocery carts full of food—in an effort to prevent a toddler from running at full giggle into oncoming traffic.

This behavior stems from a toddler's complete wonder and awe at the world. Christina can spend hours jumping into puddles just to see the ripples of the water and the change in the rainbow colors on the surface. Such pastimes are worth more to Christina than tickets to a Barney show or a trip to Disneyland.

Toddlers also seem to have a sixth sense when it comes to reading a parent's moods. Sadness can almost guarantee a hug and a cuddle; tears in a parent's eyes will bring a kind of sympathy rarely expressed in the adult world. But the most delightful trait of two-year-olds is their imagination: their fantasy world, where every girl is a ballerina and every boy a firefighter, and the sky is purple, the grass is red, and there are pirate ships riding the high seas.

In all of these ways Christina is a typical toddler. But the one "typical toddler" thing she has never done—not once— is to talk about having an imaginary friend. So I am at a loss for a logical explanation to her friendship with this man she has never met—her grandfather.

I have stood motionless by the baby monitor and listened to my daughter's one-sided conversations in which she mentions names of people she has never met and places she has never seen. She has described in detail a child's barrel chair that sat by the front door of my grandparents' home in Ohio. This was the chair I sat in when I was young and where, in its bottom compartment, I kept my toys.

I stare, dumbfounded, into my daughter's bright blue eyes as she tells me, in words too adult for her age, about a tea party she had with my father, during which he told her stories of his daddy's boats and summers spent sailing to the ocean to help the grown-up boats go home. (My grandfather ran tugboats out of Lake Erie up the Saint Lawrence River to pull freighters into port.) At times, Christina has asked me to help her dig through her toy boxes, searching for toys that I had as a child, toys long since lost or thrown away, toys that were gone years before I even thought about having my own children.

She has informed me that I have the same middle name as her "Pappa Bill," although she has never been told our middle names. Christina knows facts about relatives who died when I was a child. She recalls events and people the way my father would.

When all of this first began, my daughter almost frightened me. I recall one of the first times when I really noticed that something unusual had happened to her. It was 2:00 A.M., and I was brought slowly out of a deep sleep by the sound of Christina's wind-up musical giraffe. Assuming that Christina had somehow climbed over the railing of her crib to play—an event that my wife and I were sure would happen one day—I walked into her room expecting to scold her gently and rock her back to sleep.

I found Christina fast asleep in her crib with tears on her cheeks and her musical giraffe playing in the middle of her floor. When I had put her to bed earlier that evening, the giraffe had been on a shelf in her bookcase.

As cynical as I used to be about angels or life after death, I now only see the beautiful possibilities. I feel grateful that the one person I feared my daughter would never know now spends more time with her than almost anyone else besides her parents.

I've come to believe that these "visits," as Christina calls them, just may be my father watching over her, getting to know his granddaughter. That would be his way: quiet and comforting, practical in every sense. "Why let Christina bother Randy and Sheryl when I can help her myself?" I imagine him saying.

I've learned to cherish the peace that always seems to fill the room when I watch Christina fall asleep, and I have come to believe that the feeling is possibly God's reassurance that my little earthly angel is being watched over by one of His. So now before I turn out her light, I smile and quietly whisper, "Thanks, Dad," before going back to bed.

RANDALL CONE
Dallas, Georgia

A Christmas Prayer

*T*HE ROOM WAS growing dim. It was twilight, cold and dreary outside, and there was a chance of snow. Normally, I would've been very hopeful for snow this time of year, but tonight I didn't care about the snow or whether or not we'd have a white Christmas. Tonight, the evening before Christmas Eve, I only cared about one thing. As I sat in the chair next to the bed, I touched my child's hand, then picked it up and held it in my hand. I lay my head on the bed, put his tiny hand close to my heart, and watched him breathe . . . slow and even breaths. He looked like a sleeping angel, so sweet and peaceful.

It was hard to believe that my four-year-old son, T.J., was in a coma. And I just couldn't accept the grim prognosis given to us by the doctors. They had done all they could do, they told me earlier that day. T.J. probably wouldn't pull through this time. The infection raging through his small body was winning the battle, and all we could do was wait. As I sat in the darkening room, I quietly prayed that God would give T.J. strength to fight. What did the doctors know, anyway? This was something better left to God. Only He could save my son now.

T.J. was first diagnosed with leukemia when he was three years old. The chances of his survival depended solely on his body's response to the treatments. His was a very tough battle. Time after time his small body was pumped full of powerful chemotherapy drugs, and each time his body became weaker. He wasn't responding well. Before he'd get enough of the powerful drugs to stop the progress of his leukemia, his thin body would begin to fail in some way. The drugs were just too much for him, and the doctors were forced to give fewer drugs and smaller doses. Thus, he continued to fail. The drugs had now depleted his white blood cells and he had no other defense against this raging infection. He had slipped into a coma the day before, and the doctors predicted little chance of his waking up. "He'll just quietly slip away," they had told me earlier that day.

My mind and my heart were struggling to dismiss what the doctors had said. I couldn't just accept the death of my child. "How would you ever get past that and go on?" I wondered as I prayed again for strength. The room was so quiet and still and dark . . . and I waited.

Suddenly, out of a deep sleep, T.J. sat up in bed, looked at me, and cried, "I'm scared, Mommy, I don't want to!" I was shocked and confused. Strangely, the room wasn't as dark as it had been, even though no lights had been turned on. I asked T.J. what was wrong and what he was talking about. He looked at me, eyes wide and filled with tears, and said, "Mommy, will you please go with me? I'm afraid to go all by myself." I asked him again what he meant. He looked, first around the room, then at me and replied calmly, "The angels are here, Mommy, and they want me to go with them, now!"

My heart exploded in my chest. I sank to my knees beside the bed and began crying out to God, saying through my tears, "Please, God, don't do this—not now. I'm not ready, and it's Christmas! Please God, don't take him from me! I'm not strong enough to get through it, and he's so little." I felt as if I were at war with God: He wanted my son, but so did I. But deep down, I knew God's army was more powerful than mine.

I kept pleading with Him and sobbing, never taking my eyes off T.J. He was lying on his back looking around the room. The eyes that had been wide with fear now seemed to be gazing at something with a sense of wonder. Then he turned to me and grabbed my hand. He smiled, then quietly closed his eyes, as if he had decided to peacefully give up and slip away.

Panic gripped me. I picked him up and held him, not caring about all the tubes and IVs, and was surprised to find that he was warm and still very much alive. I sat there in the dark room holding him close, while pictures of his life played through my mind. I envisioned him sitting on my lap reading his first book, running through the wind with a red balloon trailing behind him, riding his first little tricycle, playing with his puppy, saying his prayers. My little boy had packed a lot of living into his short life, but there were so many more things for him to see and do. I wanted so badly to be able to give him that chance. But I did the only thing I knew how to do. I held him tight and rocked him back and forth. I cried and I prayed . . . and I waited.

After a few minutes, as I was looking down at T.J.'s pale, limp body in my arms, I felt the gentle presence of someone standing very near. I looked up and saw no one but could feel a certain warmth in the room. My heart seemed to lighten, and a sense of calm came over me that I had never before experienced. Then, as I looked at his sweet face in the darkness, I saw a hand tenderly stroke his cheek as he lay in my arms. As soon as I saw it, it was gone, but whatever or whoever it was left behind a wonderful feeling of peace.

T.J. remained in the coma throughout the night. The following morning, about 10:00 A.M., he slowly opened his eyes. The fever that had wracked his frail body was gone. He turned his head and slowly looked around the room. Then he looked right into my eyes and said, "I love you, Mommy," and he smiled.

It was Christmas Eve morning! What a glorious Christmas gift God had given us! Here, on the very eve of His own precious Son's birth, He had given new life to my son. God had listened to the heartfelt prayers and pleas of a very ordinary boy and his mother. And now, as I gently stroked T.J.'s little arms and hands, I glanced out the window at the brightness of a new day and I could see soft snowflakes beginning to fall.

ROBIN NISIUS
Evansdale, Iowa

My Mother's Spider Plant

I T WAS JUST an ordinary spider plant—the kind with long tendrils hanging down here and there and little baby spiderlike offshoots growing from them. I had brought the plant home when I was a teenager and left it on our back porch, never giving it another thought. After all, it was just a plant and I didn't "do" plants. But when Mom found it one day, all brown and scraggly, she immediately applied her healing touch, and the plant began to thrive under her tender loving care.

The day I left for college, Mom encouraged me to take the plant with me—something to add a little color and life to my small, drab dorm room, she cajoled. During the school year, oblivious to almost anything besides what was happening to *me*, I'd occasionally feel guilty and remember to water the plant. But *occasional* meant once or twice a semester. Every June, I'd schlep it back home with the rest of my belongings, prepared to endure my mother's wrath.

"What happened to the spider plant?" she'd ask year after year, genuinely surprised that I hadn't grown a green thumb while away at college. She never waited for my response but would promptly put it out on the back porch and start working her magic on it. And so, every year my neglect would almost kill the plant and every summer my mother would once again "bring it back from the dead."

One summer the spider plant became extra healthy, sprouting an abundance of offshoots. Mom cut off a few and in no time grew another beautiful plant, which she gave to my grandmother. It sat in my grandmother's sunny front window for years, flourishing to the point where it nearly covered the window with its offshoots.

Eventually, when the original plant was finally on its last leg due to my carelessness, Mom created a new plant for me from Grandma's offshoots. I carried the "granddaughter" of the original to graduate school with me. I always had good intentions of caring for it, but somehow my studies would take over, and nurturing a plant seemed superfluous to my academic concerns. I simply didn't have the time or the inclination.

Until my mother was diagnosed with breast cancer.

I got the news while I was finishing my dissertation at Yale. I was devastated and felt helpless being away from her, unable to help her through the cancer treatments. Suddenly, my little spider plant took on new meaning. It represented my mother's life, and I started caring for it as I would've cared for my mother if she were near. The plant quickly responded to my ministrations just as my mother responded to hers.

For the next twelve years Mom courageously battled her

disease. During that time, I married a wonderful man and we settled into a new home. Naturally the spider plant came with us and endured my erratic watering habits. We had a son and my life was full. Sometimes I'd go for weeks without watering the plant. Then I'd notice its brown leaves, think of Mom, and resolutely begin a more regular watering campaign. My mother and I lived in different states and in some symbolic way, the plant had become my link to her.

Then we got the bad news that the cancer had spread and Mom's chances didn't look good. In my sorrow and perhaps in anger, I made the decision never to water the plant again. Its life span would parallel my mother's.

And so it did. As Mom took her last breath, the spider plant withered and died, too. Not wanting to look at it anymore, I put it outside on the deck. It was March—still winter in Connecticut where we lived—and it remained cold for months after that. Snow and frost covered my little shriveled plant.

A few months later in July, I awoke from an unsettling dream. My mother had appeared to me in the dream and told me I would have a baby daughter. The dream stayed with me for days. This kind of thing had never happened to me before, so I didn't quite know what to make of it. Before she died, Mom had desperately wanted me to expand my family so that my son would have a sibling. And of course, she always told me what a joy it would be if I were to have a daughter of my own.

A few days after my dream, I was out on the deck, cleaning away old leaves and debris. As I brushed away the leaves I saw the old pot where the spider plant had once been. I gently picked it up and felt the familiar pang that came with anything attached to memories of my mother. Taking a closer look, I couldn't believe my eyes. There in the middle of the pot was the beginning of a new plant—a few tiny, bright green leaves—wondrous evidence of new life. It was a sign. At that moment I knew I was pregnant and I felt certain it would be a girl.

New life! New hope. A continuation from one generation to the next. I grabbed the pot and promised myself I would take care of this plant as never before. The plant became green and healthy as my daughter blossomed inside me. When she was born, the plant was as big and bountiful as its original mother—and grandmother—plant had been.

I still have that spider plant today. It has been a good teacher to me. I'm quite sure it was my mother's way of telling me that life goes on. That all living things—plants and people—take time to grow and achieve their potential. That relationships require patience and nurturing in order to blossom. And that my mother's legacy—the tender, loving care she gave to all things—will live on through me and my children.

And if I can only remember to water my spider plant more often, maybe I'll be able to give some of its offspring to my son and daughter when they go off to college.

LISA MANGINI
Ridgefield, CT

Camp Indian Head

H E LOOKED LIKE a lion, with his big head of bushy, blond hair, 1978-style muttonchops sideburns, and a surprisingly well-groomed beard. He was my camp counselor, and he spent every night snoring fitfully in a bottom bunk in the corner of our tiny, cramped cabin.

There were ten of us in our cabin, and we all thought the lion, whose real name was Mark, was the center of our summer camp universe.

He coached us through our swimming lessons in the tepid lake each morning before breakfast. He taught us how to organize our tubes of toothpaste and dwindling bars of soap so we could carry them easily on the way to the showers. And he quietly led us in our evening prayers before bed each night.

He also knew lots of poetry. He'd recite it to us all day long, without ever opening a book. He taught us to ride horses in the moist, smelly stables and to weave wallets out of fake leather and black twine. We learned archery under his expert tutelage and felt ten feet tall when he laughed at our corny "knock-knock" jokes.

We knew he was our friend because he told us so. "Look," he'd said on our first night together. "I'm making four dollars an hour plus free peanut butter and jelly sandwiches on this gig. That's not enough money to be faking it with you. I like you all and hope you'll like me. It's that simple."

And it was.

There wasn't much room in our cabin, but Mark made room for his rusty ten-speed, the only thing besides a couple of pairs of khaki shorts and tank tops that he'd been allowed to bring from home. He rode the bike around camp every free minute he had. When he was in one of his show-off moods, he'd ride it without hands, an art none of us measly nine-year-olds had yet perfected.

One day, he even rode it in the barn.

The barn was a combination dance hall, meeting room, and snack bar. Bleacherlike benches stretched up one side and down the other, leaving the concrete-covered area in the middle free for us hungry campers to roam, munching on Snickers and ice cream sandwiches bought with our precious snack-time account.

It was a big, wide open space perfect for dances and talent shows and announcements and riding Mark's rusty ten-speed in perfectly shaped circles.

Well, we would expect nothing less of Mark. With his biceps bulging beneath his natty tank top and his lion's mane flowing out behind him, he cycled in circles for our pleasure one day after our nature walk and before our archery lesson. We watched his hands leave the handlebars and clasp behind his head, as if he were reclining on his couch back home instead of speedily pedaling barefoot like a daredevil around a concrete auditorium. I watched in awe as his big gangly toes barely missed the spinning spokes of his ten-speed wheel time and time again.

Until, inevitably, they didn't. There was a sickening, slick wrenching sound and then the bike just stopped. The other boys from our cabin and I encircled Mark and helped him up off the cold concrete. He favored one foot, and we all gasped in horror when we saw that it was leaking a trail of blood—all the way from the barn back to our tiny cabin.

Luckily it was evening and Mark had no more counselor duties besides our nightly Lord's Prayer, which he uttered double-time, through clenched teeth.

Randy, the oldest, biggest, and wisest kid among us, suggested that our wounded leader visit the camp clinic. Mark grunted and shook his head, asking for the handy cabin first-aid kit instead. We helped Mark disinfect his wound—one worthy of any horror movie we weren't supposed to watch—and then wrapped miles of gauze around it before taping it up. By the time we were done, Mark's toe looked as big as his head!

We slept restlessly that night, all of us except Mark, who slept like a log. Moonlight filled the cabin before I finally nodded off, only to have the strangest dream of my life:

I was in a cemetery. Alone. There was a funeral in progress in the distance, but the day was gray and cloudy and rain had soaked the muddy grass and I didn't want to mess up my fancy loafers. Despite the quiet scene, my heart seemed to be beating faster and faster, as if in a panic, but above the beating of my heart I heard a continuous sound. It was the sound of raindrops, dripping one by one from the leafy tree above my head onto the ground beneath.

Drip. Drip. Drip. Over and over the sound occurred as the funeral progressed silently some yards away.

Whose funeral?

Drip.

Who was dead?

Drip. Drip.

I woke up with a start, and thought of Mark. I sat up in bed, sweaty and scared. I listened closely to the erratic snoring and sighing of a roomful of sleeping campers. There, in between the night sounds, was the same familiar refrain from my dream.

Drip. Drip. Drip.

Only, this wasn't a dream. I sprang from my bed and ran to Mark's bunk. Underneath it, glistening in the moonlight, a pool of blood was slowly spreading across the floor. The bandages covering Mark's toe were completely drenched with blood.

It took only a few minutes to rouse the clinic nurse from her private cabin, and after a rather wet jog through the early-morning dew, she was able to waken Mark and call an ambulance from the cabin phone.

Mark looked as pale as his bedsheets and drifted in and out of consciousness while we waited for the ambulance. In the meantime, the crusty clinic nurse chewed him out.

"What kind of fool goes to sleep with a chunk of his big toe missing?" she scolded him. "Why, if this munchkin hadn't had a nightmare, you could have bled to death by morning. Honest to goodness. . . ."

The paramedics interrupted the scolding and whisked Mark off to stitch up his toe and nurse him back to health. Somehow, amid all the hustle and bustle, I never had the chance to correct the clinic nurse.

I hadn't had a nightmare.

I had had a dream. A simply miraculous dream.

RUSTY FISCHER
Orlando, Florida

The Life Preserver

I T WAS A sunny yet uncommonly blustery summer day in 1998 when my son Michael and I arrived at the shore in Long Beach Island, New Jersey. We had our new metal detector and fishing tackle with us, and we were planning on another exciting father and son afternoon. It was late in the day and the lifeguards were just completing their shift as we arrived.

We weren't the only ones enjoying the beach that day. Many other families were taking advantage of the long afternoon—soaking up the last warm rays of sunshine, surfing in the uncharacteristically large waves.

Why Michael and I settled on that particular stretch of beach I don't know. I remember thinking that with the calmer water there, it was a little strange that no one else was swimming. Michael was your typical water bug, and like any other day at the beach, he had come prepared to swim. So I was surprised when he decided to dig a deep hole in the sand instead. After a while, another family settled on the beach near us—a man and a woman and their two sons, about twelve and sixteen. Both of the boys were naturally interested in what Michael was doing because by the time they saw it, the hole was at least four feet deep. My son was not quite twelve, and only his head showed above the rim.

Michael kept working on the hole—he seemed driven to keep digging—and kept asking me if I was impressed with his success at turning such a small hole into such a deep one. "Yes, Michael," I said over and over, "I can't believe how deep that hole is getting. I think you're going to reach China soon."

Eventually the other two boys lost interest in Michael's project and headed for the surf. Occasionally, I'd look around to check out how many people were still left on the beach, as we couldn't really start our metal detecting fun until most of them cleared out. When I looked up I noticed how much fun the two brothers seemed to be having as they frolicked in the water. I was feeling a little perturbed that I had brought Michael all the way to the beach and he still hadn't gone in the ocean. Instead he was now almost vertically entombed in sand. What was wrong with him today? "Michael, why don't you go join those other two boys and have some fun in the waves?" I prodded.

He stood erect, now with little more than his eyes showing above the hole and said, "They aren't having fun, Dad. They are screaming for help!"

"What?" I asked as I refocused my attention on the two boys.

"They're screaming for help, and everyone is ignoring them!" shouted Michael, more adamant now.

As I looked closer, I could see the younger boy clutching onto his brother's back. What I had assumed was horsing around now looked like something much more serious. I strained to hear what they were shouting, but the constant wind and pounding surf muffled their voices. It soon became clear to me, though, that the older brother was trying to swim to shore with his brother in tow. It looked like they were caught in a riptide and were fighting to keep their heads above water. It appeared that Michael was right: the younger boy truly seemed to be drowning.

Knowing the boys needed immediate help, but not wanting to panic, I called out to their parents, who were as oblivious as I had been to what was happening. They were sitting on the beach, very conscientiously watching their two boys, never dreaming that their sons were struggling instead of playing. Slow to react to my shouting, the mother finally responded by yelling at the boys, telling them to stop tugging on each other and to leave each other alone.

The father, too, was confused and reacted cautiously. No one seemed to understand the urgency of the situation except Michael, who kept insisting they were drowning. "Can't you hear that?" he repeated over and over. "They're calling for help." I could see now that the older boy was beginning to weaken.

The father hurried down to the water and called to the boys, who responded by splashing frantically as they yelled. Then the older boy started pushing his brother away. He was crying helplessly. We all instinctively knew that if they were truly caught in a riptide, we would only make matters worse by trying to go in after them. Their father, however, went out as deep as he could to get close to them. Finally, two men in a saltwater kayak heard the father's cries for help and were able to paddle out and rescue the younger boy, who was almost unconscious. At the same time, the father stayed in the water until his older boy swam toward him. The kayakers were then able to pick him up. A few minutes later all three lay on the shore, gasping for breath, exhausted, but grateful to be alive.

Why had Michael decided to dig a deep hole instead of swim that day? A hole that blocked out the sound of the wind, and in some miraculous way acted as a direct conduit to the voices out in the ocean? Would anyone else have heard the boys' cries of distress above the crashing waves and whistling wind? And what had kept Michael in that hole all that time—his own private "sound booth"—content to stay down there until the very moment when his voice of warning would be so critical?

I woke up the next day and realized I had forgotten to thank the Lord for using Michael as an instrument in His hands to preserve the lives of two young boys. I knew we had been in the right place at the right time, and that my young son had had a reason for doing what he did. I'll always be grateful for the pure and simple heart of a child who remained in tune with God's purposes far better than an entire beach full of adults.

MICHAEL STEIN
Philadelphia, Pennsylvania

Songs I Sang to a Dying Child . . . and the Songs He Sang to Me

I HAVE CRADLED in my arms—and in my heart—more than three hundred people as they were dying. They taught me more about living than anything else I have ever experienced. One of the first things they taught me was that when you die, you die a child. Grown-ups don't die. Grown-ups may have fatal accidents or terminal illnesses, but when it comes time to die, you die like a child.

I used to believe that when a person died there was an avalanche of silence. I was mistaken. It is more like a soft snowfall of peacefulness, a slow gathering mist quietly filling all the spaces in the room, settling quietly and gently on hearts and minds and hands that were busy. I believe this is also why we do not hear tears fall. They are absorbed by the snowfall and become part of the mist.

The first time I held a dying baby in my arms I could not stop crying. I had been called to the nursery because I was the chaplain on call, and the baby needed to be held while he died. The woman who had brought him life had also given him a terminal illness. She had gone on, leaving her newborn in the heart of the hospital and in the arms of a stranger.

I was sitting in a rocking chair. There was a screen around me. I was wearing a scrub gown. The nurse asked me if I was ready. I said yes. She placed the little warm bundle gently in my arms. My arms felt full and molded to his fragile body. He was warm. He was not moving. I pulled back the soft flannel blanket and peeked at my tiny patient's face. He wore a knit cap. I slowly pulled off his cap and watched in wonder as tiny curls and waves seemed to appear everywhere at once. His ears were perfect and his eyelashes went on forever. He puckered his lips and there was nothing left for me to do but adore him. For the next sixty-eight minutes I would live a lifetime. It would not be my own but it would change mine forever.

For the first few minutes I held him, I wasn't sure what I was supposed to do. I started to rock slowly because that seemed appropriate. It was certainly helping me, and I hoped it helped the baby, too. Then I began thinking that maybe I should hum a lullaby or pray, or say something religious. My heart was breaking. I was alone with a dying baby.

I have always told my patients and my students to say what is true. Listening hard to my own advice, I began. "My name is Vicki, and I am a chaplain. I'm sorry that your mother died and couldn't be here with you, but she is waiting in heaven, so you'll see her pretty soon. You're beautiful. You get to meet God, again. I don't have to tell you about heaven—you were just there—but I *can* tell you about the stuff you might have liked as a regular kid on earth.

"It's almost Christmas—you would've liked Christmas. I'm sorry that you'll miss all the Santa Claus stuff and the bright lights and pine smells—but you're going to the Light we celebrate. Then there is Valentine's Day. People give chocolate as a way of saying 'I love you.' But you know where true love comes from, and chocolate melts in the sun anyway. You would have liked the sun. The sun makes everything warm and feel safe—like God. But you'll have God, so maybe you won't miss the sun after all.

"You'll miss the rain, though. The rain quenches all thirsty things and brings new life like Jesus does. But come to think of it, you probably won't miss the rain very much either because you'll be with Jesus."

I gently stroked the baby's curls as I continued to speak.

"Now, the next thing I'm going to tell you about, God didn't directly create, but I personally know several reputable people—some of them are actually grown-ups—who believe that hot dogs and purple Popsicles are two of the finest foods on earth. Hot dogs require teeth, so it would be awhile before you could really appreciate them, but purple Popsicles—now there is the ultimate summertime treat!

"Imagine sitting on the porch. The sun is warm overhead. You can smell the summer smells of lawn clippings and barbecues and roses and sprinkler-washed sidewalks. You unwrap your two-sticked grape delicacy and gently take the first lick. Your tongue kind of sticks because your Popsicle is still really frozen, but that first lick has broken the barrier. You must now lick, slurp, nibble freezy bitty bites—faster, faster, until the last satisfying lick of purple leaves you with a frozen purple tongue and two smooth sticks with unlimited potential.

You put them in your pocket and promise yourself that you are going to save every Popsicle stick from the whole summer and then make something really neat, or you take first one and then the other and rub them on the sidewalk until they are no longer mere sticks but popsicle swords! Then you can do great battle with anthills and unsuspecting bugs. Your little boy fingers are covered in grape sticky and summer dirt and it just doesn't get much better."

I was rocking and talking and holding and crying and thanking God for this precious moment when I realized something was different.

I stopped rocking.

I stopped talking.

I stopped crying.

I started to listen.

All I could hear were the sounds of a busy hospital nursery in a busy hospital in a busy city on a regular weekday in November. The little person I had been holding was now an empty tabernacle. At some point in my story, my tiny listener had gone back to the heaven he came from. I did not hear him say good-bye.

When I left the nursery, I was smiling. This wonderful little creation had taught me to listen with my heart. He must have thought it was a fair trade. After all, there was nobody else to tell him about grape Popsicles.

VICKI L. BAILEY
Sacramento, California

Catherine with a C

I STILL REMEMBER THE day my beloved grand-mother and I were preparing supper together and she turned to me and said, "You know, Debbie, out of all the grandchildren I have, there hasn't been one named after me. Now, your grandpa—he has a grandson, a great-grand-son, and a nephew named after him. I guess the name Tom will be passed on down through the family for generations to come."

I was only a young girl at the time, but I could see the disappointment in her eyes. My heart ached because I was helpless to change the situation, and I would've done any-thing to make my grandmother happy. She and my grandpa lived on a farm and were the source of some of my warmest memories growing up. They were two of the kindest people I'd ever known. They taught us kids the value of hard work, yet they were never too busy to read us bedtime stories, take in a stranger, or nurse a stray animal back to health. Grandma was a small Scottish woman with a heart of gold who constantly made us feel important and loved, and whose house was always open to friends and family. I remember watching everything Grandma did—the cooking, washing, cleaning—and every mundane task was done with great tenderness and care.

And so, after my grandmother's "namesake" wish was made known to me that day, I took the problem to the wisest man I knew—Grandpa. Sure enough, he had a solution to the dilemma.

Later that day, while helping her clean up, I casually said, "Grandma, could I name my first baby girl after you?"

She didn't say anything at first, but when she finally glanced up at me I could see her tears. She looked straight at me with her clear deep-brown eyes and said, "Debbie, it would please me very much if you did that, but I want you to promise me one thing."

Ready to promise her the world if she asked for it, I said, "What promise is that, Grandma?"

"You have to promise me that if you name your first little girl after me when you grow up, you will spell her name with a C rather than a K."

I didn't have to ask Grandma why. Her name was Katherine with a K, and all her life people had called her Kate, a name she wasn't fond of at all. I had heard her complain about it for years. She knew my daughter wouldn't be stuck with that nickname if her name was spelled with a C. And so I made the promise.

Ten years later, my grandfather died and left my grandmother to carry on without him. I'm not sure which hurt more: losing my grandfather or watching Grandma try to function on her own day after day, gazing at pictures throughout the house of her lifelong companion. She had called him "Dad" for as long as I could remember. Occasionally she'd forget he was gone, and I would hear her calling him to supper.

But life continued, and a few years later I married and eventually had two sons. By this time, I had moved to a town quite a distance from my grandmother, and I wasn't able to see her very often. My sons were seven and nine years old, and my life was full and complete. But one day in January, my mother called to tell me she had placed Grandma in a nursing home because her dementia had progressed to dangerous levels. I wanted so badly to visit her, but the long trip prohibited it at the time.

Two months later, I was shocked to find out that I was pregnant. I had had my tubes tied years before, being quite content with the size of my family. Having taken this fairly permanent precaution, I never dreamed that I'd have another child. In October I gave birth to a beautiful baby girl. She was baptized Catherine Lee. Now I was more determined than ever to visit my grandmother so she would finally be able to hold her namesake in her arms. My mother tried to discourage the trip, explaining that Grandma hadn't recognized anyone—including her own children—in over two years, nor could she carry on a coherent conversation. But I knew this visit was something I had to do. I knew that Grandma would want to see her great-grandchild and would want to know I had kept my promise.

The day of the visit was quite an event. My whole family joined me: brothers, sisters, cousins, aunts, and uncles all circled around Grandma's bed. I didn't realize how much it would hurt when she didn't recognize me, but it was wonderful to see her nonetheless. I bent over to kiss her on her thin, wrinkled cheeks and then gently whispered, "Grandma, I kept my promise. This is your great-granddaughter, my little girl, and her name is Catherine."

I carefully placed little Catherine in my grandmother's arms, hoping I could at least take a quick picture of them together. Suddenly, Grandma started caressing Cathy's face and softly stroking her hair. Gazing intently at the bundle in her arms, she very clearly asked, "Did you spell it with a C?"

I could hardly speak. Somehow Grandma understood, as I knew she would. For one lucid moment, she was aware of me and of my baby, her great-grandchild and namesake. Trembling and tearful, I managed to say, "Yes, Grandma, I did." Still not taking her eyes off the precious baby, Grandma said, with great emotion, "Look, Dad. She kept her promise."

My grandmother hadn't spoken to anyone in almost two years, and after that day she never spoke another word. She died quietly the following spring, and I believe she died in peace. The miracle my family had witnessed that day would live in our hearts forever just as her name, I believed, would continue to be passed down through future generations.

Now, whenever my daughter, Cathy, asks to see the picture we took that day of her with her great-grandma, she asks me to tell her the story that goes with it. She never tires of hearing how she came to be called Catherine. I think she must know, as my grandmother did, that this beautiful name—with or without a C—holds great promise.

DEBBIE MCLELLAN
New Brunswick, Canada

God's Indestructible Word

THE SUMMER OF 1962 had been a tumultuous one for me. At seventeen, I was about to begin my senior year in high school—barely a year away from college. And already the Lord had been after me with a call to preach the gospel.

My mind was filled with confusing and contradictory thoughts. Was the call genuine? Was I just trying to please my pastor? Could I count on God to see me through this spiritual journey despite halfhearted, stingy, opinionated, and divisive church members? Was He calling me to—gasp—the mission field? Would I have to leave home, never to see loved ones again? I sought the wisdom of many counselors and read every booklet and article on the subject I could get my hands on. Still, I was perplexed.

"O God," I prayed. "If you could just give me some sort of

indication—some sign—that you will take care of me through whatever trials may come my way!"

Then came a chance to put these anxieties on the back burner, briefly anyway. My mother and I had signed up to enjoy a weeklong tour from our hometown of Huntington, West Virginia, to Washington, D.C., Philadelphia, New York City, and Boston.

A chance to get away! For a few days I wouldn't have to ponder life-changing decisions. Of course, I dutifully planned to take my Bible along—a $4.50 red-letter King James edition published by Harper Brothers of New York—and read it every day. But that was the extent of my spiritual devotion for most of the week.

Truly, the trip lifted my spirits. We rode on Virginia Trailways bus no. V217, a forty-one-passenger diesel-powered beauty with fluted aluminum siding trimmed in a brilliant red and featuring an air-conditioned air suspension ride and vast picture windows separated by those streamlined-looking slanted pillars. I could get used to that!

We saw all the sights along the East Coast—watching from the Senate gallery as politicians charted our future, climbing the heart-stopping steps of the Statue of Liberty, and boarding *Old Ironsides*. We rode the Staten Island ferry for a nickel apiece and were in the studio audiences of several network television programs, including *The Tonight Show* with guest host Groucho Marx. A devoted railroad fan, I even managed to secure a ride on the Baltimore & Ohio Railroad tugboat as she delivered a float of twelve boxcars across the Hudson River to Jersey City, New Jersey.

Preaching the gospel was far from my mind as we headed for home down the New Jersey Turnpike the following Saturday. For one thing, I was angry. I had ridden the front right-hand seat of the bus upon leaving Huntington the Sunday before—and I had liked it. So, every morning thereafter, I saw to it that I was outside our hotel first so I could throw my duffel bag on that front seat to reserve it for myself while everyone else was finishing their breakfasts. It worked all week—until that Saturday morning in Boston.

The driver was late; by the time he arrived, everyone else was outside and waiting to board, too. When he pulled up, the bus door was three feet from me. I made a dash for the door, only to be held back by my playful new friend, Colston Pitt, the tour sponsor's fourteen-year-old son. I threw my bag over several people's heads; it landed on the coveted front seat but bounced off onto the floor. Two young women—upstarts, I thought—ignored the bag and plopped down in the front seat. My mother and I had to settle for the fifth seat back, on the left. "Oh, fine." I fumed. "All I'll see today is the back of a seat." I pouted all day.

We headed toward Valley Forge, Pennsylvania, that day. By midafternoon, as we roared down the New Jersey Turnpike, some of the passengers were chatting about what we had seen, others were singing, and a few were snoozing. I was looking down, engrossed in a book I had found in a Broadway bookstore. We were now ascending onto the bridge across the Delaware River that would take us to the Pennsylvania Turnpike.

Wham!

It sounded like a blowout, but the impact was severe enough

to shove me forward, sending my upper lip crashing into that infernal seat in front of me. My mother and several others were rudely awakened to find our driver standing on the brakes in a frantic effort to stop the bus, which careened to and fro on the bridge deck, bouncing off the concrete side-wall before finally coming to rest. A wall of flame enveloped the front of the V217 and ignited along its right side from front to back.

Screaming passengers jumped up in concert when the driver ordered us out the emergency door in the rear. I paused long enough to retrieve my journal from the floor, where it had fallen upon impact. In the interim, the two passengers across the aisle from us had gotten in between my mother and me. As we made our way backward, pushing and being pushed, a thick column of black, choking smoke filled the bus. I feared it would explode before we all got off.

"So this is what it's like to die," I thought.

My friend, Colston, sitting in the rear seat, had opened the emergency door. L. T. Hicks and Charlie Bedrosian, who hit the ground first, caught the rest of us as we jumped. My mother, her arms flailing, had caught Charlie's shirt collar and ripped off every one of his shirt buttons on the way down. She was hysterical because we had been separated and she didn't know where I was. Our tour registrar, Virginia Pitt, ordered us away from the burning vehicle just as our second tour bus pulled up with its passengers gaping, trying to see if we were all right.

I looked back and saw the crumpled remains of a black sedan chewed up under the front of the bus and glanced at my watch. It was 3:08 P.M.

Our dazed driver had suffered serious internal injuries, but he had managed to help three or four of the front passengers, including the two who had grabbed "my" seat, to jump barefooted through broken windows before he passed out. When Colston went back in for our driver, he found him back in his seat, his feet still out in the aisle. Colston was a hero that day.

Sirens blared. Fire trucks, ambulances, and police cruisers arrived. Firefighters successfully removed our belongings from the underside bays and concentrated on putting out the fire.

Once the driver and nineteen injured people were evacuated to a hospital in Mount Holly, New Jersey, we boarded the second bus—fifty-eight passengers in all now—and watched the drama continue to unfold. It seemed that the Gabor family of Brooklyn, New York, had been enjoying a sight-seeing trip when their sedan, according to eyewitnesses, lost its muffler. Harold Gabor, the father, apparently swerved to the right and braked hard to stop and retrieve it when his car was struck in the rear by our bus. Sadly, all four members of the family died in the inferno. We saw one of the children's bodies being removed from the backseat. It looked like a pile of burned newspapers.

Once the fire was out, I got off our other bus to inspect the wreckage. The V217 was destroyed. Its top, except for the window frames on the left side, was gone. I walked around the right side, where I could see clearly inside, to see if any of our bags on the luggage racks had survived.

Alas, everything was gone—either damaged beyond reasonable use or incinerated. But when I spotted the seared frame of what had been our seat, my gaze intensified. In the aisle, I could identify charred pajama fragments, a vaporized toilet kit, and the skeleton of my duffel bag. There was no sign of my camera or my rolls of priceless vacation photos.

But on that seat . . .

My Bible had been in its cardboard box in my bag. The bag was gone. Everything else in the bag was gone. The box containing the Bible was gone. But there, resting contentedly on a spring of the seat, was my Bible. The binding was damaged; the gold leaf lettering was scorched away, but the Bible was there. It had survived.

No one would listen to my pleas to retrieve it until my mother glared at a firefighter with what she called her "school teacher look." Finally he got on his tiptoes, reached through a window frame, grabbed the precious treasure, and handed it to me. I could still read every word of it.

Instantly the verse came to mind: "Heaven and earth shall pass away, but my words shall not pass away" (Matt. 24:35). It was as if an angel had tapped me on the shoulder and said, "See, son? You have nothing to worry about!"

The overloaded second bus took us to hotels in Lancaster, Pennsylvania, and once a replacement bus arrived the next morning, we continued home without further incident. The trip had meant many things to us—enjoyment, education, fellowship, and safety in the midst of tragedy. But it meant much more to me—I had my sign from God. In His infinite mercy and grace, He had shielded my little Bible from the blaze that should have destroyed it—and in doing so, reminded me that if I would give myself totally to Him, He would take care of me and see me through.

Today that same blessed book sits on my bookshelf. I have been in the ministry now for more than a quarter of a century, a bivocational career that started only after years of questioning, doubting, and putting off God. But in truth the matter was decided that sultry Saturday in August, on a bridge between New Jersey and Pennsylvania, as I saw with my own eyes that a fuel-fed fire that took four lives and changed thirty-eight others could not annihilate God's indestructible word.

BOB WITHERS
Huntington, West Virginia

A Shaving Cream Surprise

URS IS A family with long and well-established holiday traditions. Every year since we were children the seasonal patterns have been the same—always the same gathering spot for Thanksgiving, Christmas, Easter, and so on throughout the year. The same people, the same delicious food, the same places. What might sound boring to some is instead cozy and comforting to everyone in our family. We know just where to go, what to bring, and when to be there—not such a bad way to live in this crazy-paced world of ours.

So where do we go when the weather turns warm? Our family camps at Lake George, New York, where else?

My father had always been the family's most enthusiastic participant up at the camp. Swimming, boating, fishing, sailing—he'd manage to get in a little of each most of the days we were there. And the campfires, the games, the barbecues—he was the one to get all those activities started and keep them going. I can picture him clearly, in a flannel shirt to ward off the evening chill, stacking the wood just so in order to build the perfect fire. My dad, like the eternal Scout leader, was our happy family camp director.

Year after year we shared wonderful summer memories. But in the last few years, I not only began to notice my own advancing age as I pulled on a bathing suit, but my father's slower pace as well. In June of 1997, after arriving at camp that very first day with his eyes shining in anticipation, he fell and broke his hip.

The local ambulance took him to Glen Falls Hospital, and the routine hip surgery went well. But the medical staff noticed a problem with Dad's blood count and ordered further testing. The tests soon revealed the extent of the problems: we were completely unprepared for the news that he had colon cancer and a large aneurysm on his heart.

And so on the Fourth of July of that year, instead of attending the annual family picnic at the lake, Dad was transferred by ambulance from Glen Falls to Ellis Hospital in Schenectady, New York, where he could be closer to his home, his friends and family, and his longtime church. The colon surgery went well, and he was transferred once again to a rehabilitation hospital to begin physical therapy for his hip.

After six and a half weeks in three different hospitals, Dad was finally able to go home. What a welcome day that was for all of us. My mother made all his favorite foods. He beamed as he sat happily on the patio, chatting with neighbors, enjoying his familiar surroundings, with the aroma of a backyard barbecue replacing the strange and sterile hospital odors. He went to bed early on the night of August 9.

The following morning my mother found that he had died during the night. Shocked and deeply saddened, we gathered and instead of discussing plans for the family's traditional fall celebrations, we planned a funeral.

Our family was incomplete now, and I didn't know how we'd ever laugh again, or even really feel joy. Dad had such a great sense of humor; he loved nothing more than to play practical jokes and make us laugh. In my fifty years I'd never spent a holiday without my father and I couldn't imagine how we'd make it now without him, particularly as Christmas approached. There were just too many things that wouldn't be the same. His musical talent was known countywide, and every Christmas Eve he would stand in the front of our little country church and play the violin to accompany the wor-shipers as they sang the traditional carols. It sounded like music from heaven. We would all miss not hearing those sweet strains this year.

My mother was even more lost than I. After a long and happy marriage, it was disorienting for her to suddenly find herself in a world without the sound of her loved one's voice, without the comfort of knowing he was just in the next room, sitting on the comfortable old plaid couch reading a book, waiting for her to join him there.

Mother and I both have been early risers for years, up with the sun and ready to start the day. I'd made it a habit to call her every morning at six-thirty, something many of my friends still can't believe. Now, with Dad gone, the calls seemed even more important. I didn't want her to go too long in the mornings without the sound of someone else's voice— I didn't want her to be alone in the house in the early morning with just her own thoughts and memories.

One morning her voice was full of wonder, instead of the sadness and loneliness I had become accustomed to hearing.

"I have a mystery on my hands," she said. "Actually, the mystery is on my floor." She went on to describe the scene. When she'd gotten up that morning, she'd found three mounds of shaving cream on the hall floor outside her bedroom door. Not small mounds, mind you, but swirling mounds of shaving cream that were almost five inches high. Where had they come from? Her house was locked up tight. Her black Labrador, Kashia, had not barked to warn of an intruder during the night. What a strange thing to find on your floor early in the morning! "I don't know, Mom. Sounds pretty weird," I said. After all, Mom was a sensible, practical woman, not one to be dramatic or wildly imaginative.

When I shared the story later that day with my son, Andrew, he said, "Mom, this is incredible! Don't you remember what Grandma told us about the last conversation she and Grandpa had the night he died? When she helped him into bed that night he said, 'I need a shave. Should I shave tonight?' And she said, 'No, it's late. Wait until morning.' And then, remember the last thing she said? It was, 'Good night, Porcupine,' because she was teasing him about his stubble . . . and then she kissed him."

When Andrew reminded me of this, I was amazed, and then misty as I pictured my mother kissing her husband good night for the last time in her life.

So, it was Dad who had left the shaving cream that night. Oh, what a sense of humor my father still had! Those little piles of shaving cream were his silly way of telling us that there is another life after this one, and that all was well. He was just in the next room after all, waiting for us to join him there.

SUSAN WHEELER
Galway, New York

Our Final Journey

OUTSIDE THE WINDOW of my mother's fourth-floor hospital room people headed for work. Cars whizzed past below us on Sunrise Boulevard, and pedestrians waited for the light to change at the crosswalk. The world was going on as usual, which somehow startled me for a moment. It was just another day—or was it?

Mom struggled to say something to me. Her throat was dry and her cracked lips could not form sounds. She had been unable to swallow liquids for two days. Determined to speak, she continued to form voiceless words. The pain of her efforts etched deep into her face. Her large eyes—like round, brown marbles—pierced into me as she battled the silence.

It took all the strength I had to keep my expression even as I tried to hide the anguish that had consumed me over the past weeks. I felt as if my guts were tangled in barbed wire and my fear was without bounds. "What will happen to her?" I wondered. I had desperately held on to the slim hope that she would not slip into darkness, though her pain had gone on far too long taking a toll on both of us. Old friends who had not seen me in a while did not recognize me when we came across each other unexpectedly at the market, until they heard my voice. I did not know what death would bring my mother and was tormented to think this once bright light would forever extinguish into a black abyss of mystery. I wondered how I could go on without her.

Suddenly, as if someone else had chosen the words I said, "Mom, don't try to say it, think it. Think it and picture what you want me to know. It will come to me. I just know it."

Where those words came from I still don't know, but they came out of me.

Weary, the muscles in my neck and shoulders ached miserably from bending over her hospital bed for two weeks. The vibrant heroine of my life, Betty Davis, whose rosy complexion and full cheeks danced around a smile for most of my life, lay in a room as gloomy and colorless as her sunken cheekbones. Her Indian brown hair had not one hint of gray. Thick and matted around her head, nurses had stated all week long, "Looks so young, and all that hair, you would never believe she was on chemo."

I lay two pillows across Mom's legs and rested my head on them. I laid my arm over hers. The pillow felt cool against my cheek. Time passed.

A tingling sensation moved up my arm and enfolded me. The weight of my shoulders, neck, and head was lifted and I became deeply entrenched in tall weeds. I rose up to see over them. Before me was an expanse of calm fields gently swaying in waves. It seemed a new dawn for light was lifting behind the trees at the far end of the meadow. Just as when one enters a door, he does not see the entire room until he is in it, the scene unfolded as I entered this peaceful place. I was taken aback by the beauty of the tall, waving grasses and suddenly the sounds of birds began to fill my ears. As with the first chirps of an awakening day, the chatter grew louder as the light grew brighter. The beauty of the scene was astounding, but the most awesome thing of all was the serenity. Never in my life had I felt such perfect peace and joy. Never.

I became aware that I was floating, because I looked down and saw the grasses passing beneath me. I was traveling with total ease toward the distant trees. I rose higher and proceeded across the ocean of reeds. As the trees grew nearer, I could see their thick, lush foliage and branches in a way I had never noticed before—closer and higher than one's vantage from the ground. The light behind them grew brighter and brighter. Brilliant! I wondered why it did not feel warm against my skin. I thought it would surely burn me, just as the sun does on a hot day. I looked over at my left arm to see if it was growing red in the intense, and yet at the same time calm, light.

There was no arm. I looked around, and there was no me. I had no physical form, yet I kept moving toward the light. As I did I passed an array of birds clasping to the thick grasses, undulating gently with the stems. Everything was so right, so wonderful, and so perfect. I did not mind at all that I had no body, I just knew that I was in the right place.

I also realized I was not alone.

When we had at last floated over the entire field, we were

lifted together over the trees. I studied the leaves and branches as they grew closer and then watched them grow smaller and smaller as we sailed higher and higher.

"I want to go as high as an airplane and see what clouds feel like against my face," I thought, forgetting I had no face. My excitement increased with the fervor of a child's Christmas morning delight.

"Let's go higher," I communicated through my thoughts to my companion. My companion's love encircled me and felt as perfect as the place we shared.

We approached a low, sparsely scattered cloud in the increasing brightness and she gave me a message: "I must go on now from here. You must go back."

I was so disappointed! No disappointment bigger than this had I ever experienced. I did not want to go back. No! I wanted more than anything I ever desired to continue, but instantaneously with her gentle command, I started to turn around, though it was not my will.

Without warning, I was suddenly pulled backward and downward, over the trees, the field, and then past the birds in the reverse order that I had first seen each one—a goldfinch, a tan-colored sparrow, a mottled one—each clinging to its reed. It was as if I was viewing a tape of my entire experience shown in reverse. I was no longer floating but being yanked back to my starting point. I still did not want to leave and thought, "I am doing this only because you, Mom, ordered me back, and I usually do as you ask, whether I want to or not. For no one else would I leave this place."

Then I realized, I had no choice. I was being taken— sucked from that wondrous place like water pulled below the surface of a drain. It had been the truest and most complete serenity I had ever felt. Why should I have to leave? Beneath me, the first weeds I had come upon were still swaying in the peace.

Slowly, I became aware of the aches and stiffness in my shoulder muscles. I felt as if I would collapse under the overwhelming weight of my own weary body. The pillow was still against my cheek. I did not move. I lay there enveloped in a rich sense of peace and harmony though my body felt like moaning.

"I'm so sorry." The words cut through the stillness like glass shattering in an explosion, though she spoke barely above a whisper.

Looking up, I was hardly able to support the weight of my head with the tortured muscles in my neck. A nurse stood at the foot of the bed.

"Your mother is gone."

Fear of the unknown often depleted my spirit during the two decades my mother, Betty Davis, struggled with breast cancer. From my teenage years, her potential demise loomed like black sky. This unexpected out-of-body miracle of traveling the path from death to the next realm with her took me from my darkest hour to the greatest experience of my life— before or since. It replaced dark with light, fear with serenity, and sorrow with joy.

From the moment of her death, countless people executed the phrase, "I'm so sorry." I would immediately reflect on our last excursion together and can honestly tell you that I was not. Our journey through death was smoother than the one through life. Though I was sad to be without her, an inexplicable calm enveloped me obliterating the grief I had experienced for so many years. When I think of miracles, I know they cannot be planned, anticipated, or comprehended, for they go beyond our own limited human minds to far, far beyond—into the limitless light.

Suzan Davis
Granite Bay, California

Miracle in the Rain

S MY DAUGHTER raced up a mountain free-way one dismal winter morning, even the fierce El Niño rainstorm would not slow her down. But when her 4Runner hydroplaned, it flipped upside down. So did my world, as I knew it.

My husband, Carl, and I inched our way to the hospital through the streams that gushed over the roadway. We had no details of the accident, only that Jennifer had been air-lifted to the hospital twenty miles away. I was paralyzed with fear, and my heart cried out, "Lord don't let my daughter die with a wall still between us."

For the past year, Jen had been on a mad dash from her problems. With her marriage falling apart, her natural spunk gave way to sparring gloves, ready to jab at any obstacle in her way. Outwardly she fought for control, but inside Jen still ached for the father who had abandoned us when she was a young teen. As I frantically tried to mend each rip in her life with a mother's counsel and correction, it only made things worse. She hadn't spoken to me in two months.

At the trauma center, the neurosurgeon told us that Jen had a serious head injury and was in very bad shape. Jen lay in a coma, her swollen, shaved head hooked to tubes, wires, and pressure monitors. Machines blipped and beeped while nurses worked frantically to keep her blood pressure stable or death could steal her at any moment. If she did survive, brain damage was likely, though we had no idea how bad the damage would be.

I knew my biggest test of faith had arrived. I met Jen's husband, Steve, down in the hospital chapel. "We had a terrible fight last night," he blurted out to me, "and I said some awful things."

As I prayed for my daughter, I remembered a verse from the Bible: "All things work together for good to those who love God." "All things?" I questioned. Even tragic car accidents?

Then it hit me. Fretting would not change the outcome. If I trusted God, I had no choice but to cast aside all doubts. My daughter's life was in His hands.

At my daughter's bedside, I prayed, "Lord give me your perspective on this. My eyes are too blurry." At that moment, she appeared so peaceful, so beautiful that I felt sure God was doing His restoration work while she slept.

Suddenly, a strange voice rang out behind me. "How's my girl?" I turned to see a young hospital technician. "Oh, hello. I'm Phillip. I was at the accident scene today with this little lady."

Then Phillip told us his story. He'd been heading down the mountain when he saw a massive billow of water several miles ahead, and a tiny dot catapult from it. He knew it must be a body—Jen had been thrown from the car as it tumbled—her body landing on the freeway just inches from the mangled vehicle.

"I was already very late to work, but something told me I had to stop," Phillip said. He told us that the highway patrol officer who was first on the scene had found no respiration and no pulse, and so he had covered Jen's curled, lifeless body with a yellow slicker. He was contacting the coroner when Phillip pulled up. "She's not going to make it," the officer said.

"I won't believe that!" Phillip shot back, and being an orthopedic technician trained as a navy field medic, he went to work on her. In a few minutes, she gasped a breath, just as another car pulled up—which happened to be an off-duty EMT with a respirator in his car!

As Phillip told us this, I pictured Jesus reaching out his arms to catch Jen, his body cushioning her against a deadly fall that should've broken her entire body. I envisioned God clearing the raging skies for an instant so the rescue helicopter could land. And I felt the peace that passes all understanding, convinced that somehow good things would come from this.

The next day Carl and I went to church, and when I opened the bulletin, I shook my head in disbelief at the sermon title: "God's Purpose for My Problems." I reflected on the fact that the way we respond to our problems reveals what we believe about God. Later, when I shared this thought with Jen's husband, he said, "Whatever happens, I know God has allowed it, and even if she is disabled, I'm committed to this marriage forever."

Friends who came to the hospital were concerned for me. "You must be in shock," someone said as I smiled calmly. "Not at all," I replied, "I just believe Jennifer is safe and secure in God's hands."

Five days later, Jen began to twitch her feet and emerge from the coma. She was not paralyzed! Excitement stirred within me. What miracle would God perform next?

I should have known. My former husband, whom we hadn't seen for ten years, showed up at the hospital. "She's just like I was," he said, "reckless and immature, running away from herself. If I hadn't walked out on you, none of this would've happened." His presence there meant a lot to Jen, as it did to me.

Ten days later Jennifer was transferred to a rehab hospital, and the doctors were amazed at her progress. She fought hard to walk again, to formulate sentences, even to chew her food. Her strong will and tenacious spirit were paying off.

Three months after the accident, Jennifer could walk shakily into her own house to her husband and two little boys, grateful that God is a god of second chances. It's been two years now, and her bruised brain continues to heal. She's still a fighter, but there's a refreshing softness about her now. "Mom," she told me one day, "I never want to be estranged from you again. I realize now how much you love me and want the best for me."

People in our small town still talk about the miracle in the rain, how incredible it was for a young woman to be thrown from her car, hurled a hundred feet, land on her head, and not just survive but recover nearly everything she had lost. They talk about the miracle of the man who refused to believe she was dead, who had faith enough to give her breath again. But there are other miracles that the people in town aren't aware of—a daughter's softened heart, her restored marriage, a family's healing. And the most wonderful miracle of all to me is to have my daughter back again as my friend.

JAN COLEMAN
Auburn, California

A Picture of Health

THE DESERT HAD never looked more peaceful as the sunset's brilliant array of crimson and burnt umber enveloped the surrounding Cadiz Mountains. First introduced to the fascinating geology and life of the desert while I was in college, I have returned many times, taking friends and family to share the beauty, solitude, and wonders of a unique world. I find a special peace in the desert where I can lie under a blanket of stars more glorious than any Fourth of July light display I've ever seen, and where the only intrusion on the silence is the occasional howl of a coyote or a couple of kit foxes inquisitively watching me prepare camp.

Each of my yearly trips to the desert holds special memories for me. One summer in Mount Carmel Junction, Utah, I stumbled across a rare ammonite fossil, more than seventy million years old. I was the envy of the thirty other geology buffs who accompanied me. On a trip to the Little Sahara Desert in Utah I befriended a stranded cat who slept two nights in my sleeping bag during the most frightening lightning storm I have ever encountered. By the third day my feline friend, Sahara, and I had become fast friends, and he traveled back to California, forever indebted to me for saving him from a life's diet of lizards and desert mice.

My spring trip was as fascinating as the others, and now it was the last day of a spectacular seven-day journey. My mother, uncle, and I had hiked Zion National Park, explored Bryce Canyon, slept on the Coral Pink Sand Dunes, mountain-biked among the amazing sand sculptures of Cathedral Gorge, and had survived an unexpected snowstorm in the Grand Canyon. This last day was bittersweet because we were heading back to the reality of our lives in Northern California the next morning.

As we sat by the campfire, savoring our last evening of desert tranquillity, I began to prepare dinner over the blazing fire. I'd saved my pasta pesto for the last night, a grand finale to the camping fare we'd enjoyed all week. When it was time to heat the sauce, I decided that I needed to use the additional single-burner propane stove I had borrowed from my friend Joe. While I stirred the noodles over the campfire, I asked my uncle, Kevin, to fire up the small second stove for the sauce. When he realized the small propane canister attached to the single-burner stove was empty, he began to remove it to replace it with a new canister. However, the old canister wouldn't come off. My mother and I watched as my uncle wrestled impatiently to remove the old can. It simply would not budge.

As I bent back down to stir the noodles, I heard my uncle mutter something under his breath, and suddenly a spray of cold propane gas exploded from the can, instantly covering the ground, the front of the tent, the side of our car, and my legs, ankles, and shoes. I turned around to see the cold gas still escaping from the canister in my uncle's hands, now making an arc over to the campfire where I was standing. In a split second, the ground, the tent, the side of the car, and finally my legs, ankles, and shoes were engulfed in flames. In the same order in which they had ignited with a roar, the flames self-extinguished several seconds later—all except for my shorts, socks, and shoes, which continued to burn. I dropped to the sharp rocky ground and rolled, successfully starving the flames. It was only after I stood up to assess the damage of the singed tent that I looked down to see that most of the skin on my legs was gone, from the bottom of my shorts to the top of my tennis socks.

My uncle and mother looked at me in horror. In shock, I sat down on the ground, staring at my charred legs, which were now beginning to ooze. "I think I'll be okay," I said, not having any real clue about the seriousness of the burn or the pain that would quickly follow.

With hardly a word, my mother and uncle began frantically throwing everything—pots, pans, utensils, sleeping bags—into the car trunk. In a matter of moments, everything—including my mountain bike and the remains of the singed tent—were haphazardly stuffed into the car. My uncle ushered me to the backseat to lie down when suddenly the pain hit me. The next hour was a blur as I lay in the back of the car, my concerned mother watching me carefully as my

uncle sped down a dusty bumpy desert road. The pain over-
took me in waves so intense that I began to hallucinate.

The first sign of civilization was an old filling station several miles down the barren road. My uncle got out and called
for help on a pay phone. They instructed him to drive me to
a Barstow hospital nearly ninety miles away. We could get
there faster than anyone could get to us. The hour-long drive
to the hospital was excruciating as I lay in the cramped back
of my Nissan Sentra, my legs swelling and oozing, covered
with first-, second-, and third-degree burns.

Days later, back in Sacramento, wrapped like a mummy
from the thighs down, I attempted to make my way around
on crutches. The swelling was horrifying. Since I had virtu-
ally no skin on my legs, I was required to change the dressings
several times a day, a job I dreaded more than anything I had
ever endured in my life.

Each day was a continual process of mustering strength. An
attempt to walk required me to stand, and when vertical, my
lower body was overcome by the enormous pressure pounding
against my charred legs. To lie down was unbearable because
the seared fascia had no protection that skin normally affords.

Every couple of days I went to the doctor to be checked for
infection. One young new nurse cried and had to leave the
room when the doctor instructed her on how to slough off
the injured dead tissue from my legs. We hoped that new skin
would grow, but as the days went by and we saw no signs of
that, there was discussion of performing skin graft surgery.

I was a young woman with my whole life ahead of me, and
the thought of being disfigured repulsed me. Having large
portions of my skin removed from other areas of my body to

patch up my legs horrified me. I simply could not and would not accept it.

A few days later my friend Joe, who had loaned me the treacherous camp stove, called to ask about my condition. When I told him about the prognosis I refused to accept, he asked me to come over to his house immediately.

When my mother dropped me off at Joe's house later that afternoon, I learned some things about him I hadn't known. He explained to me that as a war veteran and counselor he had worked with other vets, doing healing visualization techniques with excellent results. Joe asked me if I'd be willing to allow him to work with me, and I agreed.

Helping me find the most comfortable position possible in a recliner with my legs elevated, Joe began by leading me through exercises in which I imagined my legs whole and lovely again. I vividly imagined the skin intact, soft and healthy. I believed and embraced the mental images he helped me paint. At the end of the session, Joe also reminded me of the power of prayer.

When I got home, I called everyone I knew and asked them to pray for my recovery and to imagine my legs healed. I continued to depend on prayer and the visualization techniques; they gave me something to focus on other than pain and depression. Still I could not, would not, accept the probability of skin graft surgery.

A few days later at my doctor's office, after the nurse had cleaned my wounds and left, I stared at the disgusting mound of dead skin and tissue she had removed from my calves and shins as I waited for her to return with the doctor. When the doctor returned, he looked at my legs and stopped in his tracks. "I have not seen anything quite like this before. The skin is beginning to grow back in small patches. We'll hold off on plans for surgery. Perhaps your excellent circulation from teaching aerobics has something to do with it."

I shared my good news with all my friends and family. Then I called Joe.

"Keep with it, kid," he said. "I'm telling you, it works. I feel so darned bad for what has happened to you. I feel partially responsible, since I loaned you that blasted stove. I've been praying for you, too. Keep doing that visualization. It's powerful stuff, and so is prayer."

Joe was right. The next week my legs were covered in patches of pale, tissue-thin skin.

When surgery was deemed unnecessary in the weeks to come, the doctors started warning me about the likelihood of scarring. Again, I refused to accept the prognosis and embraced a picture in my mind of smooth, healthy legs and skin completely free of scars. I bathed my legs daily in herbs and natural remedies to reduce the chances of scarring, and continued to pray.

It has been ten years since that disastrous night in the desert. I still have a great love for the land and have taken many trips back to the desert, although my subsequent visits have, thankfully, been much less eventful.

My understanding and faith in God, my personal relationship with Him, and the meaning of prayer in my life have all grown to a new level. I am totally free of scars, with the exception of one tiny, insignificant blemish near my ankle.

To me, however, this small scar is of great significance because it will always be a reminder of my miraculous healing and the enormous power of love and prayer.

CARMEL L. MOONEY
Sacramento, California

About Twenty-five Cents

HEN I WAS six years old our family moved to New Mexico. My father was in the air force, and we had been stationed in cities all over the world. Our stay in New Mexico was to be a temporary assignment. I was accustomed to making friends quickly and having to say good-bye almost as fast. Sometimes that was very hard.

The first day at my new school in New Mexico I met a little girl named Jenny, and we became fast friends. We met every day for lunch and recess, playing games and sharing secrets as if we had known each other forever.

Then one day after lunch I heard Jenny crying and telling the teacher that someone had taken her twenty-five cents, which was her leftover change after buying her lunch. As I approached to comfort her, she pointed her finger at me and said, "Cathe has it, it's in her desk!"

The teacher asked me to open my desk, which I did very

innocently. And there it was—twenty-five cents in my pencil holder. The teacher asked me to return the money to Jenny, and in her mind, the matter was resolved.

I returned to my seat, heartbroken. Why would my best friend say I had stolen from her? I knew it was my twenty-five cents that had been in my pencil holder, and I knew my mother would ask where it was when I got home from school that day. In those days, a quarter was a lot of money for a child. I just couldn't figure out why someone who I thought was a friend would lie to get me in trouble.

When I got home from school and explained the situation to my mother, she was very disappointed with me. Not even she would believe me. I was terribly hurt and embarrassed, convinced that all the other kids would avoid me now. Worst of all, I had lost my best friend and didn't know what I had done to deserve it.

When I went back to school the next day, Jenny refused to play with me, and so did the other kids. It was very painful and confusing to be so lonely and isolated. Luckily, my father was soon transferred and we moved on. This time I was glad to move; I could start over and make new friends. I never heard from Jenny after that, nor did I ever figure out why she had set me up that day.

Many years later, when I was a grown woman, I sat with some friends and newcomers in a church group in California. We chatted before the official meeting began, and the conversation turned to childhood friendships. One of the newcomers began talking about how, as a little girl, she had been constantly scolded by her mother for losing the change from her lunch money. She had tried very hard to become more responsible and, in her own young mind, was making some improvements. Then one day at school she realized she had lost her twenty-five cents change from her lunch. Afraid to face her mother, she accused her best friend of taking it.

My eyes grew hot and teary as she continued saying that she would always regret that childish act because she had lost a wonderful friend that day. She had been remorseful her entire life but knew there was nothing she could ever do to make amends.

I listened carefully and watched her now-familiar face closely as she spoke. Finally, I understood why she had done it. She hadn't meant to hurt me—she was just a little child afraid of disappointing her mother!

I remained still throughout the meeting, though it was difficult to focus. I knew I needed to speak with this woman because it was so apparent that the incident had bothered her as much as it had bothered me. After the meeting was over and the other women had left to go to the coffee room, I approached Jenny. "My name is Cathe," I said with a warm smile, and I gently placed a quarter in her hand.

Jenny stared at the quarter and then slowly lifted her head and looked into my face. Tears began to stream down my face. Tears filled her eyes, and we embraced and cried in each other's arms. We were two little girls who had both longed for another chance at friendship, and now, many years later and hundreds of miles from the school yard of our youth, we were able to remember, to forgive, and to love again.

It was over thirteen years ago that Jenny and I were brought together in that little church in California. We are still good friends today. We've talked about the miraculous circumstances that allowed us to connect again and that revealed to us the importance of friendship in our lives. And now, when we hear others talk about the value of friends, we jokingly remark that "a real friend is worth just about twenty-five cents!"

CATHE ODOM
Sacramento, California

A Whisper in the Dark

OR A YOUNG girl, summers in the Panhandle of Texas were long, hot, and much too boring. At eleven I was too young to drive, and well, there was nowhere to go anyway. Most days I walked up the road until I hit the dusty dirt lane that led to my friend Donna's house. Although she was a year older, we were best friends.

She was my only friend, really. I'd moved to this little town not long before, torn away from everything that was familiar in my short life. Frightened and unhappy at first, Donna's friendship gave me something to cling to. When we discovered that we shared a birthday—July 31—our friendship was sealed.

Donna lived in a small but very tidy house on a corner near the edge of town. The white paint on the wooden frame was a stark contrast to the red dirt that surrounded it. A low picket fence reached around the property like arms encircling the little house to protect it from the harsh, hot winds that blew across the Texas plains.

Donna was a soft-spoken girl, kind and sweet, and that summer her home became a sort of refuge for me against the turbulent winds that raged through my own home. Her parents were still married, unlike my own. They were older, too, than my mother and my newly acquired stepfather. Like Donna, they were kind and quiet and comfortable to be around. I often wondered what it must be like to be an only child in this little white house with the picket fence and two kind parents who obviously adored each other as much as they loved their daughter.

Donna and I did everything together—swimming in the community pool, playing games at her parents' house, spending Saturday afternoons at the park, riding horses in the fields, and having overnights under the stars. But our favorite pastime was going on a shopping trip to the city! Oh, how we loved it when Donna's parents would drive us the thirty miles into Amarillo to go to the Sunset Mall. We could spend hours trying on shoes or clothes at Lerner's or JCPenney's, or looking at Herman's Hermits albums. Dragging Donna's patient folks in one store and out the other, we could never seem to get enough. It was on those days that I really felt as if I were part of Donna's family. It was a good feeling.

One very hot Saturday afternoon I called Donna to ask if she'd like to walk to the park with me. Saturdays at the park were a tradition—at least for everyone in town over the age of ten. With games of all sorts going on, most of the kids in town would show up sooner or later. Donna and I liked it because we could gawk at all the teenagers. The girls looked so pretty and sophisticated and the boys gave us something to whisper and giggle about. That was the real fun of Saturdays at the park. Because we were still in elementary school, this was our big chance to associate with the older kids.

The phone rang and rang that Saturday as I waited for Donna's mother to answer. No one at home? That's when I remembered: they were having breakfast at Donna's grandmother's house that morning. Guessing that they'd stayed longer than they had planned, I headed out alone for the park, thinking Donna might show up before too long. I looked for her all day, even when Stevie Ray was chasing me through the sprinklers and around the swings. I looked for her parents' familiar car, wondering what on earth could be keeping her so long. I kept thinking how much fun she'd be having if she were here with me.

Donna never did show up that day, and as the sun began to drop behind the water tower that afternoon, I knew I'd better head for home. Mother must have heard the screen door slam as I ran into the kitchen, parched and thirsty. She told me that Donna had telephoned that afternoon, just minutes after I had left for the park. In fact, she told me, Donna and her parents had driven to the park to look for me and had even driven around town trying to find me. They'd called back several times because Donna had wanted me to go with her on a spur-of-the-moment shopping trip. My favorite thing!

I couldn't imagine how I had missed her! I had walked straight to the park along the same route we always took together: through old man Wilson's field, across the church parking lot, and around the school football field. And I'd been right there at the park all day. How could she have missed me? What bad luck! It would probably be the last opportunity for shopping until school started in the fall.

I called Donna's number again just before supper—still no answer. They had probably decided to stay in the city and have a nice dinner. I was envious as I pictured all the fun Donna was having that day—without me!

Because it was a weekend and I had no school the next day, my mother often let me stay up late if I stayed in my room and didn't turn my radio up too loud. It was after ten o'clock when my mother knocked on my door. I was hanging up a poster of one of my favorite groups, the Monkees, when she came into my room. She had an awful look on her face as she sat down slowly on the edge of my bed. I immediately turned off my radio and sat down on the bed beside her. Mom gently reached out and brushed a strand of hair from my face and began to speak. "Cynthia, I was just listening to the news on TV. Something terrible has happened. Donna and her family have been in a car wreck, honey. A very bad wreck, and Donna is dead," she managed to say.

I don't remember anything else. My mother's lips were moving, but I couldn't hear her words. "How strange," I thought. "Did she say dead? Donna is dead?"

"Did you hear me, Cynthia?" Mother asked again. "Donna has been in an accident with her family. She is gone."

"Gone where," I wondered. This couldn't be true. Maybe it was another girl named Donna, or maybe another family with the same kind of car. I ran to the phone to dial her number, certain I would hear her voice. This time someone did answer. An unfamiliar voice confirmed what my mother had told me. It was Donna's aunt, and she said that not only was the terrible news true, but that Donna's father and grandmother had died in the wreck as well. Donna's mother was in a coma. It all seemed like a dream, really—a nightmare.

The next day at church everyone was talking about the accident. I was still in shock but could feel my heart breaking. There was no escaping the conversations around me, as accounts of the tragedy were repeated again and again. I felt so sorry for Donna, for her sweet parents, for her beloved grandmother. But mostly, at that moment—young as I was— I felt sorry for myself. What would I do without Donna? She was my only friend. She was the only one I could share my secrets with. She was the only person in the world who loved me just the way I was. I couldn't imagine the rest of the summer without her, much less the rest of my life.

The funeral was planned for the following Wednesday. On Sunday night Donna's aunt called to let us know there would be a viewing on Wednesday morning. She knew how close Donna and I had been, and she suggested that I come early with the family to say my good-byes. The school principal had encouraged parents to bring their children—the ones who knew Donna—to this special viewing to help them overcome their shock and deal with the death of their classmate and friend. I didn't want to go, but how could I refuse? I was her best friend, closer to her than any other person in town. How would it look if I didn't show up? Would it be disrespectful to her family? What kind of a friend was I, anyway?

I talked with my mother about it that afternoon, explaining how I felt. She agreed, telling me that I should remember Donna the way she was, not as the broken body that now lay in the funeral home dressed and made up for show. Donna had been thrown from her car, flying over sixty feet through the air, stopped only by a telephone pole. I instinctively knew I couldn't bear to see her that way. I had never experienced death this personally before and I was afraid to face it.

I was only eleven and my thoughts were still immature, self-centered in a way. I could only think of how the funeral and the viewing would feel to *me*. But as I talked to my mother, I began to understand some very grown-up things, some of which were terribly confusing to me. It dawned on me that my own life had been spared that Saturday afternoon. It didn't make any sense why Donna hadn't found me that day, but if she had, I would have been in the car at the time of the accident, too. But *that* didn't make sense—why should I be alive and not Donna? What did it all mean? So many emotions were clashing inside of me—the pain of losing my best friend, the gratitude of surviving, and the guilt of still being alive.

Mother suggested I pray for answers, asking God for help and guidance. So that night I knelt beside my bed and asked God to help me understand and know what to do, especially about the viewing. I received no answer. I prayed again the next morning, then again that night. Time was running out. The viewing was Wednesday. Why wasn't God hearing my prayers? Where was the answer I needed to hear?

Emotionally drained, I fell into bed Tuesday night. I woke in the middle of the night from a restless sleep. The sheet was pulled off the edge of my bed and my pillow was on the floor. "Oh, God," I prayed. "Why is life so unfair? Why did a nice family like Donna's have such a terrible thing happen to them? Why did Donna have to die? Why wasn't it me instead? Where is she now? Is she all right? Is she happy? Does she know I love her? Does she know how much I miss her?" Still pleading for answers, I fell back into my restless sleep.

It was her voice that woke me. In the darkness of the night I heard a small voice, a whisper really. At first I thought it might have been my mother. I sat up and looked around my darkened bedroom. No one was there. Then I heard her again. "I am all right, Cindy. I'm happy. It's so wonderful here. I miss you, too. Everything is all right with me and everything will be all right with you, too. I love you," she said.

And that was it. It didn't last long—just long enough to affect the rest of my life. A feeling of peace and comfort came over me, a feeling I had never experienced before. It was like a soft blanket wrapped around my shoulders and I was bathed in its warmth. I still didn't know why my life had been miraculously spared, but I did know that Donna was okay and that she still cared about me. And I felt a new resolve to live a life that would always make her proud to be my friend.

Pulling the sheets up over my shoulders, I drifted back to sleep, this time a restful sleep. I woke up the next morning to the smell of bacon frying. "What day is it," I wondered, confused by the activity. "Why is Mother not at work?" Then I remembered. It was Wednesday, the day of Donna's funeral. Suddenly I remembered the dream. Had it been only a dream? I had heard Donna's voice. I had heard her whisper to me in the night, telling me all the things I had longed to know, had prayed to understand. It seemed so real. I had been *awake.* I had *heard* her. That feeling of peace, the comfort of knowing she was still with me, enveloped me now even in the light of the morning.

"Time to get up," Mother called from the kitchen. As I walked out of my room I realized that I wasn't afraid anymore. Donna was all right. I wasn't upset about the viewing anymore—it didn't matter to me what her body looked like. I could remember and love Donna the way she was—alive, happy, and at peace—because now I knew she existed somewhere outside her broken body. Everything would be all right. She told me so herself.

CYNTHIA STEWART-COPIER
Roseville, California

A Love Worth Saving

WINTER IN SOUTHERN California is generally mild and uneventful, just one cloudless day after another, each blending into the next in a blur of continual sunshine. But for me in Los Angeles in 1987, winter was turning out gray.

In some ways, I was a typical young, restless woman unsure of what to do with her life. My career wasn't going much of anywhere. My family lived in Arizona, and I didn't have any close friends in Los Angeles. It wasn't a bleak life, but something was stirring inside me and I knew I needed a change. To further confuse things, there was a man in my life. Okay, he wasn't just any man. He was a wonderful, intelligent man, and handsome, too. We had grown close after several months of dating and had developed a wonderful connection. Mark and I laughed together, spent quiet time in parks, and went on long walks together. So, what was the problem?

Mark had the same problem I had. He couldn't figure out where his life was going. So there we were. I knew I loved him. I wanted our relationship to become more permanent, but he just wasn't ready. We would see each other for several days and then I wouldn't hear from him for a week. What was he thinking? Did he believe I would just wait around for him to make up his mind? I was becoming impatient with this man, as I wanted a commitment from him much more than he did.

What was there for him to figure out, anyway? Our days together were wonderful. Soft tender moments mixed with warm passion. Moments that only lovers share—those sweet, revelatory moments that bring tears to your eyes. Oh yes, we were in love and I wanted to be with him forever. But sometimes his mind seemed to be somewhere else—he was preoccupied and just not able to see our future together as clearly as I did.

It was both the best time of my life and the worst. At night, my body ached with the pain of frustration. Some days I felt so clouded with indecision that I walked for hours in search of clarity. Not knowing what to do, and anxious to get on with my life, I began to think about ending the relationship. Eventually, my frustration got the best of me, and my insistence that Mark make a decision grew fierce. My promise of moving on wasn't an idle threat, but I hoped it would motivate him in some way.

In my long waking hours, I realized I had tried every method of understanding Mark but one. So I began to pray. This was unfamiliar territory, which is why it came as a last resort. I prayed with so many questions, desperately seeking answers and reassurance. How could I stay in this stagnant relationship when I felt so strongly that I needed to move my life in a new direction? At the same time, how could I walk away from a love so wonderful?

From our long and intimate talks together I knew that Mark's mother had died when he was four years old, and that in troubled moments he sometimes prayed to her for help. Ready to try anything, I prayed to his mother as well. I needed an answer, guidance, a sign, a push, something that would allow me to get on with my life.

But nothing came. At the high point of my frustration, I found myself placing the blame completely on Mark, and we had a horrible fight. He didn't want to lose me, but he still wasn't sure where he wanted our relationship to go. He begged me not to leave yet, to give him more time.

That night as I lay in bed, tears soaked my pillow. Although Mark meant the world to me, I had to stop putting myself through this nightmare of indecision. With an aching heart, I finally drifted off to sleep.

It happened at 3:00 A.M. Out of a deep sleep I simply opened my eyes and sat up. There she was, standing at the foot of my bed, looking straight at me with an unwavering gaze. She appeared to be looking right through me. My heart was pounding. I didn't want to take my eyes off her for fear she'd disappear. The streetlight outside my window lit the room with a soft grayish hue. I could make out her appearance, although the fine details were hazy. She was beautiful and I wasn't afraid. But I instantly knew one thing: she was not of this world. She was Mark's mother.

Although I'd never seen her picture, I could see the traces

of Mark's features in her face. She was not tall, but slender and fine boned. Though her face was young, it held the look of wisdom. I could see that her hair was short, but the outer edges of her head were almost blurred. Most of all, she was lovely, truly lovely standing there in my room. In the grayness of my room I wanted to make sure that I was really seeing her. I felt my own fingers pinching the skin on my leg—hard—keeping my eyes on her as I did. Then she spoke to me.

"Be gentle with him," were the words I heard. It was not the normal voice of a person, but the words were clear. Maybe she just thought the words into my consciousness. But they were unmistakable: be gentle with him. I caught my breath. And then she was gone.

I lay under the covers, watching the dawn slowly light my window, mesmerized by what I had seen. Toward sunrise, I finally dozed off. The alarm clock shook me out of a deep sleep. Time for another Los Angeles day. I immediately remembered the extraordinary night visit. I also remembered the strong pinch I'd given my leg and was thankful that I had thought to do it. It was real. I had been given a powerful message from Mark's own dear mother. And I had received my answer. From that moment on, I decided to relax and trust in her request that I be gentle with her beloved son.

Mark and I were married a few months later. We have been married thirteen years and have a beautiful family. Through the years, I have often wondered why his mother felt so strongly that she appeared to me at a moment when I was about to abandon hope for our relationship. But after loving Mark for more than a decade now, I know what she missed by dying young, by not being there as he grew up. With strength and resolve we can only imagine, she did what she could to insure that his adult years would be spent happily with someone who loved him very much.

CHRISTINA RICHTER
Granite Bay, California

Sail Away

HE ALARM CLOCK went off at 5:00 A.M. It was still dark outside, but it was time for me to relieve my brother from the grueling all-night vigil he kept over my father at the hospital each night. Determined not to repeat another day like the ones I had had lately, I decided to go for a jog to try and clear my head before leaving to go to the hospital.

I needed a plan and I needed it today. As I ran down the quiet suburban streets, I knew my father's situation couldn't go on any longer. "There has got to be a way to help him," I thought as I ran. "I have to help my father let down his guard and go." I knew it was up to me, that my father couldn't do it by himself.

As I continued running, the idea suddenly came to me: I would use the process of visualization. Through it, I would take my father on a sailboat ride—a ride that would take him where he needed to go. My brother and I had recently tried this visualization technique with Dad to get him through an evening of intense pain. It helped somewhat, although he couldn't quite make the mental leap from the hospital bed to the stroll on a warm, sandy beach. But this time would be different.

Realizing the gravity of what was before me, I collapsed into a swing in a small city park. My feet hurt, my knees hurt, and my arms were trembling. I sat and cried deep, long sobs of loss, knowing I wouldn't see my father after today. Then, in the quiet of the morning, I looked around at the birds and squirrels getting on with their day, and I knew I had to do the same. I got up and ran all the way home, suddenly filled with an energy and resolve that surprised me. The run had been like an epiphany for me: it had provided the search, the answer, the release of my sorrow, and the return of courage.

I had to convince my father to die. I knew I could do it.

Weeks before, my doctor advised me, saying, "Death is natural; it's the dying process that sucks." At the time, I had thought his words harsh. After watching my father and our family suffer day after day, however, I realized that his words didn't begin to capture the ugliness of dying. Dad had successfully beat the first round of cancer. When it returned— even more aggressively than before—he valiantly fought it for seven more months, to his doctors' amazement. But each day for the past eleven days, the doctor had told us, "Today is the day. He will not live past today." The tormented look on Dad's face, despite the pain medication he was taking, told us he had fought the battle too long. It was time for him to release his spirit into the arms of God.

"Giving into death for a strong-willed person isn't easy," my minister had told me months earlier. "We have people who teach us everything in this world," he'd said, "but no one teaches us how to die. For someone of your father's strength, giving into dying is going to be very difficult, and you may have to help him." That morning on my run, I finally understood what those words meant.

I had once tried to talk to Dad about dying. I told him that I was only really confident about two things in life: his unconditional love for me and that there was an afterlife with Christ that I knew was better than what we had on earth. He looked at me with frightened eyes—a man finally putting his religion to the test. I knew that facing death head-on was not going to be an option with him.

Over these past months, I had come to depend on the close spiritual connection I felt with my father. We had always been "in tune" with each other: I could be a thousand miles away, yet if something was wrong or I had some news to share, he would choose that time to call. If I had a surprise announcement, he would preempt it by blurting out my news first. When he got sick, I would call to check on him, and even though he'd assure me that he was doing great, I knew better. When I entered his house, after getting on a plane and returning home unannounced, he never even seemed surprised that I had flown a thousand miles. "I knew you would come," he'd say, and I would sit silently holding his hand for hours.

When I reached the hospital that final morning, the scene was as unsettling as the day before: my father still grimacing and rigid with pain, unable to talk through the drugs; my mother and brother holding a vigil in the room as a few close friends came and went. But this day, there was more tension and commotion in the room. The nurses weren't giving the medicine my family was requesting, and there seemed to be an incessant stream of hospital personnel performing tests that were no longer necessary and which were clearly making my father uncomfortable. I could tell that my family had held it together as long as they could. I discussed the problems with the nurses and finally called the hospital administrator to get the medications we thought were necessary. Ultimately, however, I knew that we were simply going through the motions and that I needed to go ahead with my original plan.

When I saw that my father also felt the tension, I asked the others to do their arguing outside the room. Then I went to his bedside, held his hand tight, and started trying to rub the tension out of his furrowed brow. "Just try to relax," I told him, "let's go to a better place. Let's go for a sailboat ride."

My parents had owned a lake house from the time I was very young, and it was always my father's favorite place to be. He used to say that when he'd drive down the two-acre-long driveway lined with trees, he could leave the world behind. And we both loved to sail, particularly when no other boats were on the lake. "We've entered the gate and are driving down the driveway," I told him. I described the rocky driveway that had been washed out by the rains, the spiderwebs crisscrossing the limbs, and finally the woods opening onto a view of Eagle Mountain Lake. Intricately describing every detail of the view—the movement of the air, the smell of the water, and the neighbors sitting in their porch swing on the end of their dock—I helped my father fill his mind with wonderful pictures of the place he had loved for years.

Feeling his brow start to relax while I massaged his temples, and sensing his expectation of seeing the beauty of the lake, I knew I was getting through to him. "Let's go for a sailboat ride," I said, "let's just sail together." In vivid detail, I described putting the boat in the water, dropping the centerboard, pulling in the sail, and heading out at dusk for a smooth, easy sail. I let him feel the cool water, smell the brisk air, and wave to our favorite neighbors, Jim and Billy, on the end of the dock. My father's mouth, pursed in pain for weeks, softened into a full smile. I knew he was there on the lake with me. My parents' neighbor was in the hospital room with us, and she whimpered through her tears, "He's really there with you on the lake."

Dad and I continued our long, leisurely sail, listening to the soft lapping of the water against the sides of the boat. We let our feet dangle in the water and leaned back to feel the warm summer air against our faces. Dad's eyes were closed, but the look of peace and joy on his face told everyone in the room that he was where he loved being most.

It was time. Time to send him on his journey to a better place, free of pain and suffering.

"Sail away . . . just sail away," I softly chanted. "Out there beyond the horizon, Dad, sail way out there." Over and over, I urged him to sail away. As I did, his expression communicated the excitement and sheer bliss of the place where he was going.

I was holding Dad's hands when he died. I felt the joy, the physical release, and the ecstasy of him entering his eternal life. I wasn't sure what to make of it at first, but I was certain of the glory he was experiencing. His spirit was communicating to mine. "He is so happy," I burst out. "He is feeling unbelievable joy." As my family came back into the room, I tried to describe to them what it felt like: "It's better than winning the gold medal or the biggest race; it's better than getting a huge promotion; it's more exciting than the best day of your life."

My family, however, could only see death on my father's face. Understandably, they were feeling shock and grief. They didn't appreciate my uncontainable excitement. "But he's so happy," I tried to explain. "He is *really* happy." All I could feel was the beauty of the experience my father had just shared with me, and his exhilaration at meeting God. Finally, my family, in their saddened state, couldn't stand by my father's deathbed any longer, and I couldn't leave.

As I sat alone with my father, a young minister from our church whom I had never met entered the room to give his condolences to my family. I related my whole experience, what I felt, what I thought my father had felt, and how it had strengthened my faith more than ever before. Through my father, I had experienced one small moment of eternal life with God. It was Dad's last gift to me—a glimpse of eternal life, of God's presence.

This wasn't what the minister had expected from this "condolence visit." He came to give and instead received a gift. He was moved by my conviction and shared my experience with our congregation the following Sunday.

Since that time, I've related this story to many people—as has the young minister—and we have both felt its uplifting power. With all the mentoring my father did in his lifetime, I know he loves the fact that his death has helped inspire and strengthen others.

Was my final sailboat journey with my father a miracle that God intended me to pass on to others? I'm not sure. I am sure, however, that the spiritual "back draft" I felt as my father opened the door to a new life assured me that there is a good and loving God who welcomes us with open arms to a glorious place.

ELLEN REID SMITH
Austin, Texas

Special Delivery

I GREW UP IN the beautiful city of L'viv in the Ukraine. In the early 1980s I attended the University of Moscow, where I met my future husband. We married while we were both still in school, and soon after our wedding, I became pregnant with our first child.

The medical system in the Ukraine is socialized and patients can pick their own hospital and doctor. As is true anywhere, some are better than others, and it is wise to research your choices. My family and I decided it would be best to have my baby delivered in L'viv. That way, I could live with my parents as well as be near a newly renovated women's hospital. I chose a doctor whom my parents personally knew and respected.

Because I had fallen and broken my pelvic bone at age eighteen, I was a little worried that this might cause complications during my delivery. But my doctor assured me that everything looked fine, and that my relatively young age was to my advantage.

As my delivery date approached, I was naturally filled with anticipation. I was eager to have and care for our new baby, and to then move on with life as a mother, wife, and student. I was nervous, of course, but confident that everything would work out despite the potential complications. We had planned very carefully and at the beginning of September, just a few days before my due date, I went to see my doctor for what I hoped would be a final checkup. To my dismay, he said I would probably have to wait another week or two.

I went back to my parents' house that day and, feeling a great burst of energy, went on a cleaning spree. After that, I was feeling so good I went out to a movie. Upon returning home, I started having contractions but I didn't think I was really in labor because of what my doctor had told me. The contractions continued, however, and when they were ten minutes apart, I woke my parents and husband and told them the baby was probably on its way.

My parents called my doctor, but he wasn't at home or at the hospital. A nurse informed us that he was off for the next few days and was out of town. I felt my heart sink a little; this wasn't how things were supposed to happen. We called an ambulance and I was taken to the hospital. Due to strict precautions against infection, family members—even spouses— were not allowed to attend births, or even to visit the hospital room after the delivery. I was on my own through my rapidly progressing labor. After quite a long time, however, despite my best efforts, no baby appeared. I began to worry that something was wrong.

After what seemed like many hours a doctor examined me and determined that my pelvis, possibly due to my previous injury, wasn't flexible enough to deliver the baby. A cesarean delivery was ordered. There was only one problem. In order to do the surgery, the hospital was required to have blood on hand in case a transfusion was needed, and there was none of my type available.

The medical staff decided that they would try to stall my labor with medication, hoping that the right blood could be obtained by early the next day. Because of the sedating effect of the drugs, I slept through the diminishing contractions for about five hours. By the time I woke up, my contractions had completely stopped and I was no longer in labor.

Alarmed, I called for a nurse. With concern she told me that the drugs used to slow my labor had worked too well, and that they must now give me something to make the contractions resume. Blood still hadn't been located for me, and without it, the surgery couldn't be done to deliver the baby. I was transferred to a delivery room as the contractions began again, and it was decided that forceps would be used to remove the baby. Panic gripped me, but I still tried very hard to remain calm.

Just then, my nurse was called away. The hospital was filled to capacity with women in the process of delivery, and it suddenly seemed that there wasn't enough medical staff to go around. All along, I had been well attended, coached, and monitored by doctors and nurses, but suddenly I was totally alone.

Without warning, a massive contraction gripped my body.

Through intense pain, I pushed with all my strength, but still nothing happened. At that moment, I knew my baby was in trouble. I called out for someone to please come and help me. And then an extraordinary thing happened. Two very large and very dark men walked into my room and quietly greeted me in Russian. This was highly unusual because at that time, Ukraine was under Communist rule, and it was rare to see foreigners at all in our country. I had only seen a few black men in my entire life, and that had been mostly in Moscow. I don't think I had ever seen any in L'viv.

These kind, soft-spoken men quickly explained that they were medical students and that they came from a small village in Africa. They were from a long line of what would be the equivalent of male midwives and both had been trained in birthing techniques from the time they were quite young. They told me they were there to help me deliver. I was grateful for any assistance I could get at that point, and somehow I trusted these two men.

"I can see the head," one of them said, "we must get the baby out quickly." I remember them explaining, as they worked, that forceps were never used in their villages because such tools were unavailable. When deliveries became difficult among their people, an ancient practice of wrapping a long towel around the mother's abdomen was used. With one very strong man pulling on the end of the towel from each side of the mother's body, the force exerted simulated a large external contraction, and helped the mother push. With my permission, this is exactly what they did to me.

Within minutes, and with relatively little pain, my daughter was born. Her cries were music to my ears, and though I was exhausted, I was grateful she was alive and breathing. Soon other hospital staff attended me, but strangely, no one ever spoke a word to the two African men. I didn't notice when they left.

Later, after things had settled down a bit, a nurse told me how relieved she was that, with all the other commotion in the hospital, I'd managed to deliver on my own. She had personally seen a lot of damage done to the heads of babies when forceps were used and had worried about using them in my case. I explained to her about the two medical students and how they had helped me, and asked her if she would send them over so I could properly thank them. She had no idea who I was talking about.

Intrigued, the nurse asked around. No one else had noticed the men. No one knew of anyone in the hospital fitting their unusual description. No one had ever seen or heard of the technique they used to help bring my daughter into the world.

I was told that the hospital entrances were carefully monitored to keep visitors and other unauthorized personnel out, and that there were no names unaccounted for on the mandatory daily sign-in list of students, doctors, and staff.

I may never know who the two African strangers were—so far away from their home and miraculously near to hear my cry at the exact moment of my need. I may never understand where they came from, or how they got there, or why they were able to speak perfect Russian. All I know is that they came to me when I called out for help, and ministered to me with their wisdom and their ancient knowledge. Someday, I would like to tell them thank you, for without them, I might not have had such a precious and perfect gift delivered to me that day.

ELENA PELETSKAYA
Frederick, Maryland

A Little Sugar

W HEN I BECAME pregnant in 1986, it was a time of turmoil in my family because my young aunt—my mother's sister—had just died at age thirty-two, having become seriously ill while pregnant. I myself had had a difficult pregnancy with my first child, so it was with some hesitation that I announced this new pregnancy to my grandmother. She and I were very close, but she had just buried her daughter. Did she really want to hear my happy news about a new baby on the way?

Instead of turning away with sadness, however, my grandmother smiled knowingly and said, "Someday you'll understand all of what has happened. This baby will be a blessing, and the reason for her birth will be shown to you." I was much too queasy with morning sickness to try to analyze her cryptic words.

As the pregnancy progressed, it grew more and more difficult and I was confined to bed rest. During this time, my grandmother's health suddenly began to fail as well. By June, she was in critical condition and in the hospital. My mother stayed with her much of the time, sending reports home to me about Grandma's condition.

On August 11 at 11:30 P.M., I went into labor. My husband and I arrived at the hospital expecting a speedy delivery; our first child had been born in just four hours. But after two hours of normally progressing labor, suddenly everything stopped cold. I was already dilated to three centimeters, and my doctor was surprised when things suddenly came to a halt. The monitors showed that the baby was fine and the doctor said I could wait in the hospital for the action to begin again, or I could go home. It wouldn't be long, she thought, just a matter of a few hours. Exhausted, shaken, and worried about our son at home, I decided to leave the hospital.

My sister came over early the next morning with somber news. Grandmother had lapsed into a coma at 1:30 A.M. and had died early in the morning. Strangely, my labor had stopped at exactly 1:30 A.M. Sick with grief and shocked at Grandma's unexpected death, I carried my baby for another eleven days before giving birth.

Calaina came into the world a perfect, healthy, beautiful baby girl with the most startling blue eyes . . . my grandmother's eyes. At times when I fed my new baby during the night I would look down to see my grandmother's face.

Calaina was a delight and a blessing to our family, but when she started talking, things took a peculiar turn. She loved being in the kitchen, as did my grandmother. One day, when she was not quite two years old, she was in the kitchen with me as I prepared sweet corn for lunch. Calaina looked up at me as I was stirring and said, "You know, when I did the cooking, I used to put a little sugar in it." I was stunned. My grandmother had always put sugar in her sweet corn, as she did in just about everything she cooked. Many times she'd tell me she had "doctored it up a bit and put a little sugar in it."

About a month later, we were again in the kitchen when Calaina matter-of-factly said, "You know, I always wanted you to live with us." I was caught off guard because my grandmother had always expressed that wish to me. I turned and looked down at my tiny toddler and asked her, "Who?" She answered simply, "Why, your grandpa and me, of course."

Many other unusual things continued to happen throughout Calaina's childhood. Grandma had been a big Elvis Presley fan; my daughter loves him, too. From the age of two she would become completely still if she heard his voice on the radio or on TV. She could always pick it out. When she was three she asked if she could go see Elvis Presley and cried when I explained that he was not alive.

Grandma had been a country singer when she was young, and Calaina always stood and demanded an audience every time she sang. She never played ordinary instruments like other young kids; she took drumsticks and guitars and turned them into my grandmother's favorite instrument—the fiddle.

Calaina always wanted fancy clothes and had a "pretend" microphone in her hand most of the time. She cringed whenever she heard someone sing off-key. My grandmother's pet peeve was when someone sang "flat."

My daughter is fascinated by cardinals, and my grandmother had collected pictures and sculptures of that very bird.

When Calaina turned nine last year, she started packing her daddy's lunch every day. I never asked her to, or prompted her at all, but I wasn't surprised when she started to do it on her own. My grandmother once told me that she had begun packing her own father's lunch when she was eight.

I'm not sure what all of this means. Did my grandmother foresee her own death the day I told her about my pregnancy? Did she already have knowledge of the fact that people can continue to communicate, though they are "worlds apart," if the bonds of love are strong enough? I don't know, but I do know that her words are still awe-inspiring to me.

For, the truth is, Calaina has been a wonderful blessing to all of us. She sustained me through the grief of losing my grandmother, and she is a constant reminder that Grandma lives on. Whether it's her preoccupation with the song of cardinals or reminding me to add a little sugar to my cooking, I see Grandma's loving smile twinkling in Calaina's eyes every day.

CYNTHIA UNDERWOOD
Penn Run, Pennsylvania

Never Alone

M Y FATHER DIED of cancer and my mother died of emphysema. I, like them, was a very heavy smoker. When I was quite young, I had the sense of smoking being glamorous—the faint print of lipstick on a filter, the flicking of gold lighters, and Daddy lighting Mommy's cigarette.

When I was a little girl, I could find my mommy in a store by following her cough. When I was a teenager, I stole cigarettes from my parents and hid in the bathroom. I stared into the mirror as I learned how to inhale. When my adolescent baby fat embarrassed me in the presence of my spaghetti-thin friends, I learned that cigarettes could cut my appetite. When I felt anxious in social situations, I found that a cigarette gave me something to hold on to. I literally hid my shyness behind a smoke screen.

Years later when smokers became outcasts, clustered outside buildings in wind and rain, smoking promoted camaraderie. Smoking was an excuse to strike up a conversation. Outside every building exit, gathered around the entrance to every shopping mall, I found a ready-made group of friends.

Before my father's death, long before my fortieth birthday, I developed a trademark smoker's cough. I was chronically short of breath. On vacation alone I struggled to carry my suitcase and struggled for air on a train platform. I would hurry to the end of the platform so I could get a seat in the smoking car but then, lighting up, I knew my days of independent travel were numbered.

Within a week of Dad's death, I was in bed, exhausted. Desperately trying to sort out how I'd be able to take care of my mother, deal with my son, and handle a demanding job as a social worker in a maternity home, I sensed Dad standing on my front porch one day. I knew there was something important he was trying to tell me. I wasn't sure I wanted to hear it.

As the year passed, my mother became progressively weakened by her own grief and a decade of emphysema. Her face rigid with pain and anger, she would ask me, "Do you want to be like this? Do you want to end up like me? If you keep smoking, this is what will happen to you." I stared at my shoes and fidgeted with the lighter in my blazer pocket. I wanted to sneak outside for a cigarette while she lectured. Only smokers know the feeling.

My mother soon joined my father. I discovered that it doesn't matter how old, how competent, or how educated you are; when your parents die you are an orphan. I was an orphan whose hair was starting to turn gray—a middle-aged weepy orphan who sat up night after night filling ashtrays and reliving the past. In my memories, my parents were young, vital, strong. They moved energetically, spoke excitedly, looked toward the future. I couldn't recall when my parents had stopped looking forward to the future.

Then my mother invaded my dreams. I would see her, frail and shaking, struggling for air. Gasping, Momma said, "You have to quit smoking, please! You'll die like me." There were tears in her eyes.

Later it was Dad who came to me. He reminded me of all the things he had wanted to do and put off until it was too late: fun things, family things. I kept dreaming of a day that occurred a few weeks before Dad died. He and mom were sitting in their chairs. Dad said, "Remember the first trip we took to Cuba?"

Mom, usually talkative, simply nodded.

"Do you remember the restaurant in Miami where we had hearts-of-palm salad? It sure was good." Dad smiled. They were both silent. No more trips, no more plans.

I started feeling my father's presence more and more. I would feel my heart pound and an electric energy course through my veins. It was like being on emergency alert.

I was the emergency. He was trying to get through to me. I had to quit smoking.

So I set a date. Two days before the date, I woke up scared and angry. Only two days left as a smoker and I didn't know if I could do it. I had smoked all my life. I had used cigarettes to stave off boredom, disguise shyness, and provide the illusion of contemplation. I kick-started my days with caffeine and nicotine and eased my nights with smoke. How could I possibly give this up?

I thought of walking through gardens. I thought about my own garden—full of tasks and rewards. I remembered how much I'd once enjoyed swimming laps and blushed when I thought about the last time I tried to swim. I couldn't swim, or dance, or take real walks; I smoked all day instead.

Then came the miracle. The day before my quitting date, I woke up feeling cushioned in love. I had dreamed of my parents and Mom had said, "I will lend you my strength." Dad had held me in his arms and said, "We'll be right there with you." They were giving me in death the strength they couldn't give me in life. I felt enormous relief that this would be my last day as a smoker.

For the first time, I felt calm, strong, prepared. The next morning I woke early. Curled up in bed I listened to birdsongs and traffic noise. I watched the dawn seeping through the blinds. I didn't feel alone. They were there, both of them. Mom and Dad, who had sat through endless plays and piano and dance recitals cheering me on, who had consoled me through divorce and advised me through graduate school, were with me now, at this most important graduation of my life.

I got out of bed knowing I could beat the urge. I felt cocooned by love. When my nerves jangled and the craving hit, I felt my mother telling me it was only a craving; it would pass in a minute or two. Later in the day, frustrated and short-tempered when my computer mysteriously balked, I found myself wanting a cigarette. "And how would a cigarette fix your computer?" I heard my father ask.

The three of us got through the first day.

Occasionally, through the hardest periods of quitting, I'd think of rewarding myself with a cigarette for doing so well in the process. But I'd immediately feel my parents' reaction. Supported by their firm love and compassion, I did not succumb to my addiction.

I began looking to the future. I smelled the flowers in my garden and walked around the neighborhood. I found things to do with my hands. My life was full of firsts: my first meal in a restaurant without a cigarette, my first long drive without one. I felt young, like a little girl learning to walk for the first time, seeing the world for the first time, and my parents were by my side with every step I took.

I was a three-pack-a-day smoker before I quit. I am a nonsmoker today and will be a nonsmoker tomorrow. As addicted as I was, nothing short of a miracle could've turned me around. My parents came to lead me through the difficult climb to health and hope. Their love has given me a new chance to live out my intended years instead of wheezing myself into an early grave.

Miracles that save lives are not always dramatic rescues; sometimes they are simply brought about by the guiding hand of love. So, why me? I'm not special or gifted or particularly worthy of rescuing. But just when that thought enters my mind, my father's gentle voice and wise counsel come to me loud and clear: "You are special and worthy of a miracle because you are loved."

DIANE GOLDBERG
Charlotte, North Carolina

Holding Charlotte's Hand

T HE SUN WAS shining on July 23, 1989. People were planning picnics and lounging on the beach. But it was that same beautiful day that my husband and I sat in a room at the end of a hospital corridor listening to the news that our eleven-year-old daughter was going to die.

Charlotte had primary pulmonary hypertension—a rare heart-lung disease—in its advanced stages. The doctors did not expect her to see autumn, let alone Christmas or the New Year.

It's funny how your mind wanders back to all the "firsts" with your child when you know that every word, every act, might be her last. I recalled the first time Charlotte's little hand had slipped trustingly into mine five years before. She was my stepdaughter—the child of my heart, if not of my flesh—and I was determined not to let her down now when she needed me most.

The hospital psychologist had encouraged my husband, Terry, and me to be open and honest with Charlotte about her condition and to invite her to talk about her feelings.

"Are you afraid of dying?" I asked her one August afternoon.

"Sometimes," she said. "But then I just close my eyes and I see this little cross away in the distance. Then I feel really peaceful and I'm not afraid anymore."

Days became weeks and weeks became months. Charlotte's need for supplemental oxygen went from occasional to constant. Her body bloated and the skin broke open on her legs where fluids seeped out. She needed morphine and far more care than we could provide, but with in-home nursing assistance, Charlotte was able to remain at home.

Autumn came and went and we were granted one more Christmas with our little girl. A big treat for Charlotte was our church's annual Christmas pageant. Afterward, as I wheeled her out of the sanctuary, Charlotte tugged on my sleeve.

"Mummy, Mummy, I saw it again! Only this time it was close up. I saw the cross close up!" Charlotte said she had seen a wooden cross resting on a cloud, engulfed in sunbeams. At the center was a pink carnation—Charlotte's favorite flower—wilting and dropping its petals into the cloud.

A week later Terry's brother, Andy, was visiting. After hearing the description of Charlotte's vision, he asked to see a Bible. Andy opened it and Charlotte smiled serenely as he read aloud. The verses compared a believer's death to a seed being planted in the ground. What springs forth from the seed is nothing like the seed itself, but is glorious in comparison. Our heavenly bodies will be like that, it said, more beautiful than we can imagine (1 Cor. 15:35–44). It was a comforting thought for all of us.

With the new year Charlotte's pain and frustration increased. In severe pain, she became a tyrant, verbally bullying her brothers and nurses. The weeping edema of her legs and feet was a constant irritation, and we began to be on the lookout for bed sores.

Every few weeks Charlotte had to be taken to the hospital to be drained of the excess fluid that made breathing even more difficult for her. This was a painful and gruesome procedure that involved lancing her side and inserting a latex tube, and then emptying container after container of fluid from her body.

In the spring of 1990 new life bloomed all around us even as death drew nearer. We were tired. We were angry. The day of Charlotte's comforting vision seemed lost and long forgotten. Her "cross" was looming in our minds, but it no longer seemed to be supported by sunbeams. Terry was working that April night as I tossed and dozed on our sofa bed. Charlotte was dying and all I could think about was the possibility of her slipping away when I wasn't there to hold her hand. I confessed that fear to her once and she said, "Don't worry, Mummy, you'll be there," as though there was no question about it.

The night nurse finished checking Charlotte's vital signs, made sure her oxygen tank was working properly, and went into the kitchen to fix herself a cup of tea while her patient slept.

"Charlotte." A voice called to my little girl.

Her eyes popped open. It was a man's voice.

"Daddy?"

Her name was spoken again and she looked over at the chair next to her bed. An indescribable figure in luminous white sat there. He continued to speak to her—loving, comforting words that brought peace and joy to her heart. When she told me about it later she was completely serene.

That afternoon Charlotte received a card in the mail and squealed with delight when she read it. "That's what *he* said to me! That's what the man in white said! I knew it was something from the Bible."

"Fear not, for I have redeemed you," the inscription read. "I have called you by name; you are mine!" (Isaiah 43:1)

On April 20, 1990, with all fear erased, Charlotte drifted into a deep, peaceful sleep. Her name had been called by someone who knew her well, someone who had already comforted her in a way I never could. And as she had predicted, I sat next to her, holding her small hand in my own, confident now that as her life slipped from my hand, it was being held securely in His.

TERESA ARSENEAU
Sarnia, Ontario Canada

Just Another Sunday

MY HUSBAND STARED at the photograph of his father, shocked at the resemblance. It wasn't too surprising that David's reaction to the photo was mixed. He felt the strange excitement of seeing for the first time an older version of himself, but at the same moment, there was the familiar pain of knowing he had been abandoned by this man almost twenty-four years before.

David and I had met on a blind date a couple of years earlier and had felt an immediate connection. Through the months of dating, we shared the various stories of our growing-up years. The first time he told me that he had never known his biological father, I could feel the deep hurt and resentment in his voice. All David knew about his father was his name: Lary Lampert. His mother didn't even have a picture of David's father, so David had grown up feeling completely unconnected to the man who had given him life.

We were married in September of 1992 and just ten months later, we welcomed our own baby boy, Zachary, into our lives. As David experienced the new role of father with his little son, it was at times bittersweet. He couldn't help but reflect on the contrast with his own upbringing. Now more than ever he wanted to be acknowledged by his father. But how?

David began by searching for a picture. He finally found one through a friend of his mother's who had kept in touch with Lary through the 1970s. It was a start. Next we checked the phone book and other local phone listings, but came up with nothing. It was a slow pursuit and time went by with no leads. Still, the obsession to find his father continued to plague my husband.

One day, in October of 1994, shortly after our second anniversary, we were attending our usual Sunday morning church service. We arrived a bit early, and after we were seated, I watched as people continued to stream in until the church was full. It was just like any other Sunday, sitting there in the large church among a congregation of approximately three thousand people. As we stood to sing a hymn, I casually glanced down at a Bible that lay on the seat in front of me. A name was delicately engraved on its front cover: Maria Lampert. My heart started to pound. I touched my husband on the sleeve and pointed to the Bible. He glanced at the name, then quickly looked up at me. "That could be my sister!" he whispered. Could it be that easy, we wondered. Could the clue to finding David's long-lost father be sitting right in front of us?

The service ended. David took a deep breath. As the woman in the pew in front of us turned around to pick up her Bible, David reached across the pew and touched her on the arm. She looked up at him. "Excuse me," he began, "but I noticed the name on your Bible. Are you Maria Lampert?" She seemed a bit puzzled but replied that she was.

David continued, "Do you happen to know a man named Lary Lampert?"

"Well, yes, my dad's name is Lary," she responded, "but why do you ask?"

We stood together in the church as David explained his story of not knowing anything about his real father other than his name. She replied that she had not seen her father in about sixteen years, as he had moved to Missouri in the late 1970s. They traded questions and answers for several minutes but couldn't find anything that connected the two names. She graciously offered to meet us at 3:00 P.M. that day at her home to compare pictures. It seemed to be the only way to see if there was a connection. As she and David exchanged phone numbers, each of them blurted out at the same moment, "He worked for the phone company." Then they just stared at each other. Maria's hands began to shake as it became apparent to both of them that something more than a mere coincidence was taking place. David fought back the tears all the way to the car.

We arrived at Maria's home a few minutes early. We sat outside the charming little blue house and said a prayer that God's will would be done. Taking a deep breath, David rang the bell and Maria welcomed us in. She explained that after she had arrived home she called all the relatives who might know anything about whether Lary might have a son. She had even tried to call Lary himself, but there was no answer. "Well, there's only one way to find out!" I said as I gently placed the pictures in her hand. "That's my dad!" she gasped. She began to cry. Tears filled David's eyes. "That means that I'm your brother," he said softly as he walked toward her. They exchanged an emotional hug, one that was long overdue for David.

As they wiped away the tears, the questions poured forth and the photo albums appeared. Maria filled David in on a brief history of her life with Lary. Maria's mother and Lary had divorced in 1966, and Lary had met David's mother in 1967, so Maria was David's older half sister. After a couple of hours of reminiscences, the puzzle pieces were finally fitting together. Even though Maria hadn't seen her father in many years, she kept in touch through phone calls and letters and so suggested that she call Lary with the news.

Maria didn't reach him until later that evening after we had left. Shock led to tears as she broke the news to her dad. "You can talk with David yourself tomorrow night if you'd like," Maria offered, "they've invited me over for dinner." With great emotion, Lary replied, "Yes, I'd like that."

The following evening our doorbell rang and we welcomed Maria and her sons into our home. Dinner was ready, but no one felt like eating. After some small talk Maria asked, "Are you ready?" David nervously responded, "Okay, let's do this." They dialed Lary's number.

Lary and Maria chatted a few minutes, then she smiled and

held the phone out to David. He pulled up a stool and placed the receiver to his ear. "Hello?" he said tentatively.

"Hello," a deep, familiar-sounding voice replied. In an instant, tears were streaming down David's face.

"I've waited twenty-five years for this phone call," David confessed to Lary. The conversation lasted several minutes as Lary inquired about David's life. David was beaming as the two men explored uncharted territory together. They talked and laughed, agreed to send pictures, and finally, reluctantly, hung up. David was euphoric. It was more than he had ever hoped or prayed for.

The rest of the evening was equally memorable, especially when Maria shared an astonishing fact about the Sunday morning we had met her. She asked if we were aware that originally she had been seated on the opposite side of the congregation. Then inexplicably she had felt compelled to get up and move to the other side of the church. That was when she moved to the pew right in front of us! God had brought us all together in His perfect place and time. How fitting that it was even His book that revealed the name we had sought for so many years.

Several years have passed since that Sunday morning. Lary has come to visit us, and David has traveled to Missouri to spend time with his father. Life for David has come full circle. The anger that was buried deep in his heart has dissipated in the healing light of his newfound family. He continues to be a wonderful father, letting his children know how much they are loved, both through his words and through the time he spends with them. For David, the role of father will never be taken for granted. Through the miracle that brought his own father home to him, David realizes more than ever the importance of a father in every child's life.

Teri Brinsley
Antelope, California

Grandma Dolly's Kitchen

M**Y GRANDPARENTS' OLD** abandoned Arkansas homestead for years was reported to be haunted. Although I never would've dared to go there at night, here we were, driving out one day under the hot July sun. Safe enough, I figured. The dilapidated old house was destined to be burned to the ground in a few short months, and my aunt (who had grown up with nine siblings in the old wood frame house sitting on several acres of farmland and forest) wanted to see it one last time. My husband and I had come from California for a visit and had agreed to take my aunt to the place that held so many memories for her.

We drove out on the roads she knew well. We had planned to take a last look around, take some pictures, and collect a few keepsakes before the house became a pile of charred wood. This place had been part of my father's heritage and I wanted to preserve some memories of it.

As we walked into the house, we saw cobwebs everywhere and piles of crumpled newspapers all over the floors. A low buzzing sound alerted us to a hive of bees in the outside wall. The furniture was long gone, but there were other unusual signs of life, all looking as though they'd been left in exactly the place where they had last been used—jars of home-canned food, my uncle's old army uniform on a hanger, a mattress, old trunks. There was nothing of value, but each item seemed to hold a lifetime of memories, especially for my aunt.

Rummaging through a trunk in the back bedroom, I found two letters written by my grandmother to her sister, describing the epidemics that were raging at the time. Her words were full of agony over the death of her husband and worry over her baby's illness. That baby was my father, and although I hadn't known my grandmother well, I suddenly felt a connection to the courageous woman who had struggled all alone in this house to care for her ten children. Tucking the letters into my pocket, I felt as though I had just met my grandmother for the first time. I wanted to know more of her.

My husband and my aunt went upstairs, walking carefully to avoid the litter and the holes in the floor. As they poked through old books, I decided to explore the kitchen area. I knew it had been the center of family activities and that my grandmother had spent long hours cooking there each day. This was the room where she had lovingly provided nourishment to body and soul for my father and so many others. I knew that if I could feel her presence anywhere in the house, it would be in the kitchen.

A few old spoons and an old teakettle lay on the floor amid other debris—not much evidence of Grandma Dolly's devotion to her family. Just off the kitchen I noticed a little porch that I couldn't remember ever seeing before. It looked charming, overlooking trees and brush and open fields. I could picture Grandma stepping outside there to cool off from the kitchen's heat. I tried to open the door. It wobbled but wouldn't budge. Strange. I pushed again. I could see a crack of light around the door, could feel there was no weight holding it closed, but no matter how hard I shoved and pushed, it held absolutely firm. My husband and aunt heard my attempts and came down to see if they could help. Even with the force of three people, it seemed that the more we pushed, the more the door resisted.

My aunt suddenly turned and walked into the bedroom off the kitchen area. A window looked out onto the porch from the bedroom, and my aunt gasped as she saw what was on the porch floor. "Oh, thank God!" she whispered. There, just outside the door, was a huge copperhead snake. It had heard my banging and was coiled to strike. My knees went weak as I realized what would've happened if the door had opened. The snake lay exactly where I would have stepped. With crumpled papers and debris covering most of the porch floor, I never would have seen him!

My aunt, a hearty and brave woman, grabbed an old hoe, opened the bedroom window, and somehow was able to kill the snake. Still quaking in my shoes, I walked back to the door off the kitchen and pushed it tentatively. It swung open easily. None of us could speak for a moment, reeling from the impact of what had just happened. Silently we acknowledged that something incredible and unexplainable had taken place.

To this day, I don't know if it was Grandma Dolly trying to protect her careless grandchild from harm or an angel sent to hold that door firmly shut. But the three people who witnessed it will never doubt that a miracle took place that day—a heaven-sent miracle that saved my life and filled all of us with deep gratitude.

LYNNE SWARTZLANDER
Vancouver, Washington

Together at Sunset

*M*OST PEOPLE LOOK at a sunrise and think of hope and faith, of new beginnings and good fortune, of God's original promise to His children. But to me, the ultimate symbol of hope and joy is a sunset, for it was a glorious sunset that helped me make one of the most important decisions of my life. Every time I look at an orange and gold sky at dusk, I think of David, and I am grateful. Let me tell you why.

Many years ago when my children were two and four, I found myself in a hopelessly crumbling marriage. The eventual divorce was hard on all of us. The aftermath left me feeling hopeless and confused about the future for me and my little girls. Asking God for help or direction somehow seemed wrong, since I had severed the marriage vow I'd sworn in His presence. Did He still love and care about me? I needed His guidance to show me the way.

Months went by. And then I met David.

He was a gentle, kind, encouraging man who came into my life as a friend. Over time he wove himself into the fabric of my little family. I'm not sure when it happened, but our friendship evolved into something more meaningful. There were quiet dates, family outings, and eventually, there was love. David was wonderful not only to me but to my children, too. He made us all feel cared for and loved. But my doubts still prevailed. I had convinced myself that believing in "happily ever after" was for other people—not me.

After dating David for two years, I realized that my doubts and fears were keeping all of us—David, the children, and me—from moving on with our lives. I knew how much David wanted a wife and children and how much he had to give to a family. If it wasn't going to be with me and my children, I needed to let him go so he could seek someone else and build his life with her. It wasn't fair to any of us to let things continue this way.

About this time, I began to have very restless nights. I'd never had sleep problems before, but for several nights in a row I woke up suddenly at 2 A.M. and then was unable to go back to sleep. Alone in the dark I would obsess over my relationship with David. Where were the answers? I sought help from above. "Please give me the answer, God. Let me know if I'm meant to be with David."

I continued to silently pray for help that second day as I packed the car for a trip to the coast, where David had invited us to go camping with his family. My continual inner prayer was for guidance. I simply needed to know. That night, I found myself suddenly awakened again at 2 A.M. It was the third night in a row. Snuggled deep inside my sleeping bag, I tossed and turned. I could not continue with my life this way any longer. There, in the chill of the night air, I asked God for a sign to let me know whether David and I should continue our relationship, whether we should eventually marry. In the darkness of my tent, I made an even greater request of God—I asked Him for a sign but requested it before the sunset of the next day! Looking back, I realize how bizarre and presumptuous that seems. I was asking the Lord of the Universe to meet my urgent demands on my schedule, but He knew the intent of my heart. I only wanted to do the right thing. In my first marriage I had trusted my own judgment, and that marriage had failed. This time I was determined to let God show me the way. I loved David deeply, but I was willing to walk away if that was meant to be.

Throughout that following day, I kept my prayer request a secret, hidden deep inside my heart. Every so often, though, I would gently remind Him, "Please show me what to do—on this very day—before sundown. Please!" I didn't intend to be disrespectful, I just knew this was the very last day I could go on like this. I had no idea what the sign would be, or what direction His answer would take me, but I knew it would be for the best.

The day lingered on. It was pretty much uneventful. I was still waiting, watching. Several of the family members camping with us asked us to join them on a walk. David asked me to stay behind with him to talk. My heart began to pound. This must be it, I thought. My sign is finally here. Was David going to tell me he wanted to end our relationship? I braced myself as I searched his face for sadness or pain. Instead,

David took my hand in his, looked into my eyes, and started sharing his feelings about how happy he was to have me there at the coast with his family. It should have been a beautiful moment, but with my mind so consumed with receiving an "answer," I'm afraid I didn't appreciate it for what it was. In my anxious state, and with the day getting late, frankly, I was beginning to feel a little annoyed. Where in the world was my sign from God? The sky would soon be dark and my future was still so clouded. Had God simply forgotten me, or was I simply being childish with my demands?

David and I continued talking as we began to walk toward my children and the rest of his family. I stared at the ground, kicking at the sand as we strolled. I heard voices chatting in the distance, and as I looked up, there stood David's whole family, my girls among them. They were in front of us near the sea cliff. "They must be admiring the beautiful ocean," I thought.

When the assembled party saw us, they separated down the middle to reveal a small table covered with a white linen tablecloth. In the center was a vase with beautiful flowers. On either side were two long-stemmed glasses and a bottle of champagne. It was quite a picture, but I was so preoccupied with my own impending "sign" that I almost missed it when it was right in front of me.

David led me to the table and pulled out the chair. This was all for me! Trembling, I sat down. David went down on one knee and pulled a ring box from his pocket. It was incredibly romantic, straight from a movie scene. But as amazing as it was, and as much as I loved David and all his carefully orchestrated plans, I felt panicked. I had made a promise to

God that I would make my decision based on His will alone. Now, here was David on one knee with all his relatives watching, the deadline was almost up, and I still didn't know what my answer should be. My obstinate mind simply didn't recognize what God was so graciously trying to show me.

I was here. It was now. David's proposal hung in the air. What would I do? Closing my eyes tightly, I turned my head away from him and caught my breath. I fought back the tears. With my head still turned I opened my eyes. It was then I beheld the most beautiful sight. A magnificent sunset on the ocean's bed filled my vision. As my eyes scanned that glorious horizon, a calmness filled my soul. I heard a soft, still voice say, "My child, you asked for your sign by sunset."

TERI BRINSLEY
Orangevale, California

"Remember"

I GREW UP in an angry home. My earliest childhood memory is of holding tightly to my teddy bear, listening to the sounds of my parents' loud arguments. Where is my sister, Laura? I hear something loud and bad and I look toward the kitchen doorway. Daddy is in the doorway, shouting at Mommy, and Mommy is flying through the air toward me. Daddy looks so scary. Mommy thumps onto the floor, crying and holding her arm. Daddy is shouting. I need to run . . . run!

I always connected fear with my father. "Shhh . . . don't talk too loud, Daddy might hear . . . Don't talk at the table, Daddy might get mad . . . Don't talk in the car, Daddy might get mean . . . Daddy might hit me." Even on the few occasions when he held out his arms to me I would not go to him. I wanted my Daddy to go away, to go away from all of us. Then we could be happy.

For twenty-eight years, I wished my father would go away. Finally, he did. He died a very prolonged and painful death from cancer in October 1988, with my sister, Laura, and me by his side. By his side? I don't know why we were, really. I suppose somewhere inside all of us we wish for a loving relationship with our parents.

As I sat next to my father's hospital bed I tried to tell him that I wished everything had been different. My voice choking with emotion, I tried to ask him, "Why?" Why had he always been mean? Why had he always been so angry? Why were his bottles of liquor more important than my brother's Little League games, than our school plays, than our family love?

His body was completely swollen and he struggled for every breath. I knew he heard me: even as feeble as he was, he became agitated as he lay there in the bed. My old fear returned, and I backed away from the bedside of a man so weak from disease that he could no longer do me any harm. Still, I was afraid.

Did he have the strength to answer my questions? Would he finally apologize to Laura and me and tell us how much he really loved us? No, he did not, and he passed away at dawn.

Soon after his death, I became engaged. I married the following May and went from being a city girl to being a wheat farmer on the high plains of Nebraska. It was so quiet out there on the farm. So peaceful. So unlike the household I'd grown up in. Here was my chance to make the kind of home I'd always longed for.

A farmer's day is a long one, and my husband was out for long stretches of time. I was often home alone "setting up house," putting away wedding gifts and getting the kitchen to look just so, daydreaming of the wonderful family life we would have. But odd things began to happen. If this was my big chance to build the happy life I'd always wanted, what was I doing backed up in a corner of the room, feeling so terrified? Why was there yelling all the time inside my head? I couldn't admit these feelings to anyone and I didn't have close friends there to confide in anyway.

One night in late summer, I'd just nodded off to sleep in our bed next to the big open window. From our warm bed, I loved being able to watch the stars over the wide-open plains and breathe in the smell of the wheat and native grasses. It was so unlike my cramped little childhood bedroom, so much healthier, so much happier.

In the midst of my peaceful sleep, suddenly there was an angel over me. The angel looked at me very intently, and I understood I was to go with him. We entered a place that was filled with golden light, and as we walked forward, I saw another angel—a very tall and authoritative angel—waiting for us, a serious expression on his face. Power radiated from him. He was dressed in a luminous white robe and his hands were folded in prayer. I could feel his continual prayer. Standing next to this angel was my father. He was dressed in a charcoal gray business suit and had a thick, full head of blond hair. During my lifetime, his hair was sparse on top, but pictures of him as a young man show a full head of blond hair.

I also saw two straight-backed chairs facing each other. My father was looking at me with an expression on his face that I had never seen while he was alive. From his demeanor I felt his complete remorse, love, and plea for forgiveness. The tall angel waved us both toward the chairs. Once we were seated across from each other, the angel turned to me and said simply, "Tell him."

I knew what he meant. I immediately shouted, "I am so angry!" As I did so, the angel surrounded my father and me with his enormous wings. I don't remember what happened next to my father but suddenly I knew I was standing alone before the tall angel. As the golden light in our surroundings shimmered around us he said very distinctly to me, "Remember, the most important way to live is with love—only love—and by serving others." As I walked away accompanied by the smaller angel, his voice once again echoed, "Remember."

I woke up just as dawn was breaking. The birds outside the window were calling, and I was lying on my back with my hands clasped tightly in prayer. I looked at my sleeping husband to see if he knew I'd been gone, but of course, he had been asleep.

I was overcome and awestruck. Drained by the vivid dream, the overwhelming feeling of love stayed with me the rest of the day and infused me with new strength.

With that dream, my life completely changed. Perhaps it was just something conjured up by my subconscious, but I don't think so. It felt like a gift from heaven. I was finally able to put away a lifetime of anger at my father and my childhood sorrow. The screaming voices inside my head quieted. One brief moment of being able to express the true feelings of my heart to my father had washed away much of the anger, and allowed love and forgiveness, like waves of warm, clean water, to wash over me.

I realized that day that if each of us could have an angelic experience as vivid as this one, the peace of God would fill the world. I went on to build the family that I always wanted as a child, a harmonious and loving home in which my husband, my children, and I can thrive and grow. And every day, I remember the message the angels gave me: remember, live with love—only love—serving others.

Kristin Linton
Dalton, Nebraska

The Right Door

T ALL HAPPENED so quickly. My mother had had heart surgery and was recovering at home. Things seemed to be progressing, except for the fact that she never got her voice back in the weeks following her operation. Through whispers, she tried to let us know what she needed, and everyone did all they could do to make her comfortable. Our concern grew in earnest when, at a certain point, she began to get weaker. No caretaker, nurse, or doctor could explain what was happening. In the sixth week following her operation, Mom passed away.

The idea of our family without Mom was, to us, an oxymoron. We had always been so close-knit; Mom was the center of our universe and the inspiration in all our lives—the glue that held us together. In the months just after Mom's death, I prayed hard and fervently to see her again, to hear her voice and to feel her wonderful presence. The first few dreams I had in the ensuing months were not the ones I had prayed for, however. They were worrisome dreams filled with images of Mom hooked up to tubes and machines, as she had been in the hospital following her heart surgery.

Nonetheless, small things happened in my life that gave me pause and made me feel that she was there with me when I least expected it. The most bizarre event happened one day when I was in her kitchen, cleaning, and heard the doorbell ring. My parents' poodle barked, as always, and I walked to the door to open it. I looked out to the security gate to see who the visitor was before "buzzing" in him or her. To my surprise, no one was there. So I went back inside to resume my cleaning.

Then a realization struck me. My father had told me that the doorbell had broken the day before and was still inoperable. Indeed, I remembered seeing the doorbell wires protruding from the wall when I had arrived that day. I suppose I could've felt frightened that the bell had rung, but for some reason, I was comforted by what may have been a reassuring message from my mother that all was well. A gentle feeling of peace came over me.

The greatest solace came when the dream I had prayed for was finally granted. One night about six months after Mom's death, I experienced in my sleep a type of soothing warmth that started from my head and continued to my toes. A vision appeared of my mother in a room filled with a golden glow. She was sitting at a sewing machine and had a little babushka tied around her head. She wore a housecoat, as she often had at home in the mornings, and she looked up and smiled. I nearly jumped out of my skin with joy at seeing her as the serene feeling enveloped me. I was so grateful to have been able to see her. I knew that I would remember every detail of the experience for the rest of my life. I said hello, and she also responded with great happiness at seeing me. I asked her how she was, and she said, "Oh, just fine," as if we were just chatting about the weather.

"What is it you're doing there?" I asked, as I saw her concentrating on the item she was sewing.

She replied, "Oh, I'm making wall decorations."

"What do you mean?" I queried.

"Look over there," she answered. I turned to see an entire wall lavished with intricate embroidery in ornate patterns and swirls of color. At the time, I wasn't surprised at seeing the wall; it felt already familiar to me, which seemed rather odd when I reflected on it later.

I wanted to know more. "So, what's been going on, Mom?" I asked.

"Well," she said contemplatively, "I went through the right door. Not everyone is going through the right door, you know."

I was astounded by her statement. "Like who, Mom? Who didn't go through the right door?" Then she uttered the name of a friend of hers and my father's whom I didn't know very well. The revelation didn't make sense to me, however, because this particular man was still alive. I had heard he was ill but certainly not near death. I shrugged off her comment and bid her a friendly farewell as I slipped into another stage of sleep. The warm feeling from her presence stayed with me into the waking hours.

That morning I opened my eyes with a contented smile on

my face and told my husband of my "visit" with Mom. Because he had loved her dearly, too, he was pleased that I had been given this gift, and hoped it might happen again.

We were both disappointed when that didn't happen. Although I had dreams that included her, none compared to that glorious moment with my mother in front of the decorated wall as she sat at her humming little sewing machine.

Several months later, my father called to tell me that the family friend of whom Mom had spoken in my dream had passed away. I was saddened, and inquired about the funeral services. He told me that the funeral would be simple. This man had never embraced religion; he had rejected his family's faith and had led his life as an agnostic. There would be no church sacrament, no priest in attendance, and no words of a life beyond at the funeral. There would only be a few people making speeches about their memories of him.

I immediately recalled my mother's prophetic words. What door was he going through? Why had he chosen the wrong one? What did it all mean?

I don't pretend to know the answers but can only surmise that perhaps those who choose to live without faith may not have sufficient divine knowledge to pass through the "right door." I murmured a quick prayer for the soul of this man who my mother had already anguished over many months before.

In the days and years since, this memory of my mother has comforted me more than any of the material possessions she left behind, and the vision of the "right door" infuses me with faith. It strengthens my belief that people and events in life are connected in spiritual ways—ways that can act as stepping-stones to bring us all to a higher level of existence.

And somehow, I am reassured that when my time comes, my dear mother will be the first one to greet me as I have the privilege of walking through the same door she chose.

Dena Amoruso
Folsom, California

Angel on the Fourth Floor

OW WELL I remember the moment I began believing in angels. I was ten years old and living in Melbourne, Australia. My grandfather had been taken ill unexpectedly and admitted into Cabrini Hospital in Malvern.

Each day for four days my mother and I would visit the hospital after I arrived home from school. And each day Grandpa didn't seem to be any better. In fact, my mother came away from the last visit wiping tears from her eyes. That's when I realized Grandpa had to be really sick. Mom never cried in public.

On the fifth day Mom dropped me off at the curb outside the main building of the hospital, as she had done previously. "Go on up, honey. I'll be there in a minute."

"But, Mom, can't I wait for you?" I pleaded. I didn't want to go in without Mom. What if something dreadful had happened to Grandpa?

Mom shook her head. "It may take me a few minutes to find a parking space. So many people are here today. I'll meet you on the fourth floor." I watched as the car quickly disappeared behind neat rows of parked automobiles. With a heavy heart I made my way to the hospital elevator. When the doors opened, I entered and pushed the button for the fourth floor. Leaning against the elevator wall, I recalled our first visit to the hospital four nights before.

I'd crept into Grandpa's room and stopped short. A rumpled white sheet hid most of him. As I tiptoed closer, I noticed his face was even more wrinkled and pale than I remembered. I reached for his hand on the coverlet. My small fingers closed around the limp and gnarled fingers. They felt cold in mine. Then I noticed the plastic tubing running from his arm to a drip on a stand by his bedside. "Could this really be my grandpa?" I wondered. The steady beep, beep of a heart monitor echoed in my ears. I gazed into his face, drawn and still, on the pillow.

What had happened to the grandpa I'd known? He'd always been there for me, as long as I could remember. Ever since I began school Grandpa had walked me to the stop to wait for the school bus. He'd be there again to meet me at the end of the day. It felt so good to see his smiling face and outstretched arms, especially if my day hadn't gone too well. Then just five days ago when he wasn't at the bus stop, I'd known something had to be wrong. I raced home to find Mom waiting for me. "Where's Grandpa?" I panted. "He wasn't at the bus stop."

"I had to take him to the hospital," Mom said. "Doctor White wants to do some tests."

"Tests? Like at school? Is he going to be okay?"

"We'll go and see him tonight," Mom said, ignoring my question. Later I had overheard Mom talking to Aunty Ruth on the phone. "Dr. White has admitted Dad into Cabrini Hospital. He says it's touch and go." I didn't quite understand her words, but I guessed from the tone of Mom's voice that Grandpa wasn't doing too well.

Standing there in the elevator, I bit my lip and struggled to hold back tears. Grandpa couldn't leave me behind. He just wouldn't do that, I told myself. Who would meet me at the bus stop? And if Grandpa didn't wake up today, he'd never even see the red roses I was holding that Mom and I had bought to brighten his room.

"Are you visiting someone, too?" a gentle voice asked beside me. Startled, I glanced up. A tall man wearing jeans, a T-shirt, and sneakers looked down at me. He had white-blond hair like a surfer and the darkest brown eyes I'd ever seen. When he smiled, his face lit up just like one of the angels on a Christmas card.

I nodded. "My grandpa. He's sick."

A smile spread across his face. "They're beautiful roses. I'm sure he will like them."

I frowned, glancing at the velvety red petals. "My grandpa's so sick he probably won't even know I brought them," I said. I felt a lump in my throat and swallowed quickly. I didn't want this guy to see me crying. I turned my face away, toward the corner of the elevator.

"I'm sure your grandpa will be just fine," the man said.

I shook my head. "Mom doesn't think so."

"Really?"

"Mom told Aunty Ruth it was touch and go."

"Aunty Ruth?"

"I heard Mom talking on the telephone," I said.

The man was silent. I clutched the flowers closer. What if I got all the way up to the room by myself and Grandpa wasn't there? What would I do then? More tears welled up. I needed to get out of the elevator. Suddenly the elevator stopped and the doors opened.

"Good, fourth floor," the man said, holding the doors. He turned back to me, looking deep into my eyes as he reassured me. "When you see your grandpa today, I'm sure you'll find him much better." His brown eyes sparkled under the light and there was a calm smile on his glowing face.

"Really?" I said.

"You can count on it." With those firm words the man strode out of the elevator.

"Gee, thanks, Mister," I called to him. But he didn't even glance back. Disappointed, I hastened to the elevator doors and peered out. The long corridor was empty. Where had he gone?

"Looking for someone?" a familiar voice asked. I turned. Mom was getting out of the other elevator.

"Did you see the guy who was in my elevator?" I asked. "His eyes just twinkled and twinkled."

Mom shook her head. "I didn't see anyone," she said, taking my hand. "Listen, dear, you'll need to be very quiet. Grandpa's probably sleeping. He's been sleeping most of the day, the nurse tells me."

"But, Mom, the guy in the elevator said Grandpa would be all right. He says I can count on it!"

Mom shook her head. "I'm sorry, Rosemarie, I just didn't know how to tell you. Your grandpa might not get well at all. He is very, very sick."

"But the nice man on the elevator—the one with the pretty eyes—he said . . ." Mom stopped and placed her fingers over her lips. "I don't want to hear any more about it," she whispered.

At the nurses' station, Mom paused. "Excuse me, did you see a young man with blond hair pass this way? My daughter says he stepped out of the elevator she was riding in."

The nurse shook her head. "The only person who's come down this hall is Dr. Stafford, and he certainly doesn't qualify as a young man."

"Are you sure you didn't see him?" I asked. "He had the nicest brown eyes and friendliest smile."

The nurse shook her head. "Sorry."

Outside Grandpa's room I paused and peered in. Grandpa's eyes were open. I crept shyly toward him. "How are you feeling, Grandpa?"

"A little tired, but much better now that you're here. Are those roses for me?"

I nodded. "See, Mom? The man was right."

"What man?" Grandpa asked.

Mom shrugged. "Rosemarie insists she talked to a man in the elevator. But I didn't see anyone. I just asked the nurse on duty, but she didn't see anyone, either. I think the poor girl is just tired. She needs to get her rest."

"But, Mom, Grandpa—the man looked just like one of those angels on Mom's Christmas cards." I ran to the door and peered out. Maybe I would catch a glimpse of him leaving. "Could he be . . . an angel?" I wondered, staring down the empty corridor. And do angels really ride elevators?

It was just the beginning—the beginning of a belief in miracles. In my heart that day I understood for the first time that wonderful miracles can happen to anyone—even to a little girl who was no longer afraid of losing her beloved grandpa.

ROSEMARIE RILEY
Fresno, California

A Scientific Mind

"Everything in the universe is conserved," my scientist husband once told me. "Water is conserved; no new water is actually made, it just cycles through. There is no new air. Things simply change. Everything is conserved, nothing is wasted. So why not the soul?"

The soul? What did a scientist know about souls?

We met over science, actually. I was the teaching assistant in a nuclear chemistry class at the University of Southern California; Ed was a graduate student. We met, we dated, we married. And then for thirty-four years we lived together in a quiet suburban neighborhood, side by side with other quiet suburban families in neat ranch-style houses. Did we still talk about science? Did we ever again talk about souls? Not really. We were far too busy with our lives, his as an engineer with Aerojet, mine as a teacher and the mother of our two children. Intellectual musings about the workings of the universe were of little significance in our world of career challenges, report cards, and leaky roofs.

And then, after three decades together in our comfortable house and with our comfortable family, Ed died.

I wasn't thinking of his soul when he died. What soul? He was gone, that's all I knew, leaving me alone in our house to grieve without anyone to talk to about it. Mixed with that grief, though, was anger. That was normal, I suppose, but it surprised me. I felt real anger at my dead husband for leaving me to deal with life and its problems. Things he had always taken care of—balancing the checkbook, unclogging the toilet, fixing the sprinklers—were now up to me, and I was angry. Since the day I had first seen him across the classroom at USC, Ed had woven himself neatly into my life, and now I didn't know what to do with the broken, fragmented threads he left behind.

Ed's habits had changed just before he died. Too weak to do much, he had taken to watching hour after hour of television in our family room, a habit he once disdained. Too much to do, too much to learn, no time to waste on inane TV shows, he had always said. I liked that about him. But after he died, I took up the habit myself. I was depressed and trying to escape my own loneliness. Each night in my empty house was just like the next: TV show after TV show melded into one another until one continuous laugh track filled the room.

Ed had been gone for three months when one night I suddenly felt that there was someone else in the room with me. It wasn't just me and the actors and the canned laughter. There was a warm, tangible presence in the room.

I turned and looked toward the living room. What I saw has stayed crystal clear in my mind ever since. There was my husband, Ed, at the end of a long hallway of light. He was walking toward me, dressed in his favorite pair of brown slacks and cotton shirt. The warm light behind him seemed to be guiding him—pushing him—toward me down the hall. It was bringing him to me, bringing him back into my life after these long, lonely weeks. But why was he coming now? After three months, although my grief remained, the anger had subsided. I was beginning to make small strides toward healing and bigger strides toward being able to handle the mundane details of life on my own.

Ed continued to approach me through the tunnel of light. I was awestruck, dumbfounded, confused. I felt as if I were being paid an unannounced visit from an estranged lover, and while I wanted to embrace him, I also feared being vulnerable to the pain of losing him again. What I finally said surprised me:

"Go home, Ed."

Go home? Why was I urging his spirit—this obviously "conserved soul" of my husband's—to leave me alone?

"Go home, Ed," I said to him again, gently this time. His expression never changed; he looked at me with complete love, not hurt. He understood what I meant before I did. The golden light from the long hallway behind him began to fade, and then the image disappeared entirely.

My scientist husband had been right all along. Nothing in the universe is wasted; everything is conserved. Ed's soul had returned to me that night to urge me to move on. And in the peace that came from knowing he was okay—that his body was now free of pain and disease—I knew I'd be fine without him. I could let him go. I could handle things now—the leaky faucets, the car repairs, the checkbook, even the being alone. And I could also face life on my own now.

In that single lovely moment in my family room, it was my own emotions that were recycled and my own heart that was changed.

LILYAN MASTROLIA
Sacramento, California

$\mathcal{A}$ C K N O W L E D G M E N T S

S WITH OUR earlier "miracle books" we are deeply grateful to everyone who has been so helpful to us throughout the entire process. Working on these books has been a four year odyssey of wonder and joy that we will always treasure. Words cannot express our affection for our agent, Sheree Bykofsky, our editor, Toni Sciarra, and her assistant, Katharine Cluverius.

Hundreds of people have shared their stories with us over the years. We'd like to thank the following for helping make this book a reality: Dena Amoruso, Teresa Arseneau, Vicki L. Bailey, Teri Brinsley, Shelley L. Bereman-Benevides, Jan Coleman, Randall Cone, Cynthia Stewart-Copier, Suzan Davis, Carmel L. Mooney, Karen C. Driscoll, Rusty Fischer, Diane Goldberg, Hilary Hinkley, Kris Kelly, Nikolaus Kozauer Ph.D, Judy LeSeuer, the Lewis family, Kristin Linton, the Miller family, Lisa Mangini, Lilyan Mastrolia, Debbie

McLellan, Lucy McGuire, Marie Foley Nielsen, Robin Nisius, Cathe Odom, Elena Peletskaya, Barbara Pitcavage, Christina Richter, Rosemarie Riley, Ruth Rocker, the Sander family, Ellen Reid Smith, Michael Stein, Lynne Swartz-lander, Cynthia Underwood, Susan Wheeler, Bob Withers.

Do you have a miracle you would
like to share? We are putting
together more books about
miracles. We would love to hear
about the miracle in your life.
Please send your story to:

JENNIFER BASYE SANDER
BIG CITY BOOKS
"MIRACLES"
P.O. BOX 2463
GRANITE BAY, CA
95746-2463

Please include your address and phone
number so that we can contact you.

6/04   12   3/04
8/08 (18) 1/08
11/09 (19)

11/10   21   9/10
11/12 (26)
4/18 (28) 5/17